The Geometry of Well-Being

The Geometry of Well-Being

A Structured Path from Ambition to Inner Freedom

Ramesh Srinivasan

Geometry of Well-Being Press

ISBN 979-8-9956776-1-1

www.geometryofwellbeing.com
ramesh@geometryofwellbeing.com

To my parents

Table of Contents

Preface

For more than twenty years, I have been a collector of observations. I kept notes on purpose and duty, on free will and destiny, on creation and death, on sorrow, joy, and calm. I was guided by a quiet conviction that life, when lived with clarity, can offer a *steadier* form of Well-Being—one less dependent on circumstance.

These notes were never meant to become a book. They were private attempts to understand life as it shifted across different roles and phases. I wanted to make sense of what allows a human being to live with *steadiness* and *dignity.* Each entry belonged to its own moment. Over time, many early views felt incomplete. Yet each was an honest step toward the truth.

Friends and family encouraged me to publish these reflections. They sensed these notes might help others navigate their own paths. I hesitated. The hesitation was not about clarity; it was about authority. I am not a spiritual master. I do not claim arrival at any final state. My interest has never been in offering answers. It is in understanding *patterns*—what works, what fails, and why.

By training and temperament, I am an engineer. In computer science, when a system fails, we do not guess. We look at the *architecture.* We look for the *constraints* and design assumptions that limit performance. We ask what *friction* can be removed.

When it comes to our inner lives, we abandon this logic. We treat Well-Being as a "mystery"—something that arrives on good days and evaporates on bad ones. We rely on vague advice to "be positive" or "let go." We rarely stop to understand the *mechanics* of why we feel stuck.

The turning point came earlier this year. My elder son, Sayuj, said to me simply, "You have to write a book." Something shifted in that moment. The work no longer felt private. It felt worth offering.

I knew I did not want to write another book on "how to succeed" or "how to be spiritual." The world does not need more instructions. It needs better maps. It needs tools to help us see where we stand, and why we struggle.

This gap—between how rigorously we approach external problems and how casually we approach our own Well-Being—led to the core insight of this book.

Well-Being is not a *mood.* It is a *geometry.* It has *dimensions.* Just as physical space is defined by Length, Width, and Depth, our inner state exists along three specific *axes:*

- **Length (Engagement):** How fully do we participate in life—or do we merely endure it?
- **Width (Identification):** How far does our concern extend—or does it stop where self-interest ends?
- **Depth (Stability):** How stable is our peace—or does it rise and fall with circumstances?

When we understand the geometry of where we stand, judgment gives way to clarity. We stop calling ourselves "lazy"; we see a constraint of Length. We stop feeling guilty about being "selfish"; we see a system operating with narrow Width. And we realize that "burnout" is not a moral failure. It is the inevitable result of high Engagement trying to survive without Depth.

This book offers two things.

First, it introduces a framework to assess your stability at any stage of life. Second, it presents a structured map of growth. These are not moral rankings or spiritual hierarchies. They are simply states that offer increasing *structural integrity* over time.

Many of these stages—ambition, ethics, contribution, contentment—have been explored individually. But they are rarely shown as a *system.* We need to understand how they relate to one another, and why certain stages reliably support a deeper peace than others.

The aim is not to demand belief or radical change. It is to support progress with clarity. The goal is to help you see where you are, identify the *constraint,* and see what allows Well-Being to expand. No leaps of faith are required. You only need honest observation and lived testing.

I offer this not as a teacher on a pedestal, but as a *fellow architect.* I found a *blueprint* that made sense. I offer it here. If it helps you reduce *friction* and build a steadier life from ordinary days, it will have done its work.

— Ramesh Srinivasan

Acknowledgments

This book did not emerge from a single tradition. It took shape over many years at the intersection of lived responsibility and professional work, deepened by reflective inquiry and spiritual exposure.

The framework stands on its own. It was derived through observation and lived testing, and can be examined on its own terms—without adopting any of the traditions that quietly influenced its development. Yet it was shaped by people who influenced different dimensions of my life, and they deserve acknowledgment.

I am deeply thankful to my parents. They shaped the emotional and moral soil long before I ever thought of writing a book. My father embodied simplicity and ethics. He lived with a quiet dignity. He never spoke of scarcity. He never imposed expectations. He refused to measure success by outcomes. His decency remains a silent compass within me. My mother's life is an expression of strength. She sets aside her own comfort without hesitation. She pours unconditional care into everything she does. Her resilience without bitterness and service without display are gifts I am still learning to fully receive.

I am grateful to my siblings—Sukanya, Sumitra, and Venkat (Suresh)—each of whom, in different ways, model responsibility, warmth, moral clarity, and quiet excellence. Their lives expand my understanding of standards that do not seek recognition.

To my wife, Vini—the love of my life. Thank you for your companionship and trust. Your presence has been a silent anchor. You held the ground through every phase of my life, and through the long process of shaping this book.

To our elder son, Sayuj. His discipline and clarity of priorities continue to inspire me. His simple words—"You have to write a book"—were the spark. They transformed private reflection into shared work.

To our younger son, Shreyas. He embodies simplicity and inclusion. He lives without judgment. He reminds me daily that openness is not learned through theory. It is lived through presence.

I also acknowledge the distinct influence of my professional life. Engineering trained me to think in systems. Years spent working with structure and constraints, optimization and first principles, taught me to look for the clarity beneath the complexity. These habits of mind shaped the framework presented in this book.

I am thankful for Jahnavi, a dear friend who left this world too soon. Her life instilled in me a sense of urgency to live consciously. She taught me that compassion and forgiveness are not ideals. They are necessities for inner growth.

I am grateful to Jagadambika Alisa, a dedicated teacher of classical Yoga. Her emphasis on discipline and consistency supported a period of deep inner reorientation. It continues to influence my relationship with attention.

My sincere thanks to Sriram, Priya, Joan, Vijesh, Radhika, and Mark, who generously served as early readers. Their thoughtful feedback refined the language and tone. They improved the book's accessibility in ways that mattered more than they may realize.

The philosophical underpinnings of this framework were quietly shaped by years of reading in the Vedantic tradition—its teachers, its texts, and the lives of those who embodied its insights. I have not named them individually here, because the framework this book offers is intended to stand independently of any tradition. But the debt is real, and I am grateful for it. Among those who shaped this foundation early was Sri Hemachandrudu, who came to our home during my teenage years and opened the world of Vedantic inquiry to me. That early exposure planted questions this book has spent decades trying to answer.

To all those whose names I may have missed but whose presence or quiet influence shaped this journey—I remain grateful.

Above all, I am thankful for life itself—for its challenges and tenderness, its disruptions and clarity. It has been my most consistent teacher.

With humility, I offer this work as an expression of gratitude for all that I have received.

The Map and the Journey

Most of us don't ask, "Am I enlightened?" We ask something simpler and closer to home: "Am I doing well?" We ask it of our work, our relationships, and our inner selves.

Well-Being is the most fundamental human wish. We want to feel *steady* within ourselves and connected in our relationships. We want to be purposeful in our work, and able to rest at night without the persistent hum of anxiety. Yet despite how central this wish is, most of us move through life without a clear way to understand what actually supports Well-Being over time.

This book offers a map. It is not an answer sheet; it is an *orientation.* It begins exactly where you are—with your responsibilities and constraints, your ambitions and commitments intact. It offers a structured way to understand how Well-Being can grow within ordinary life, step by step.

What makes this map different is not the promise of new ideals. It is the provision of a *lens.* Using this lens, you will be able to discern for yourself why one stage of life tends to be more stable than another—and what actually changes as Well-Being deepens.

Note: *If this framework initially feels theoretical, stay with it. In the chapters ahead, these dimensions are applied to ordinary life, and the geometry quickly becomes concrete.*

The Problem We Rarely Name

We live in an age of extraordinary precision. We research endlessly before buying a laptop. We compare specifications and read reviews; we watch demonstrations and debate trade-offs. We scrutinize cooking oils and sleep routines, fitness plans and investment strategies. For even modest decisions, we seek data and structure before acting.

When it comes to the most fundamental of all human needs—our Well-Being—we proceed by instinct alone.

We rely on vague advice and borrowed beliefs. We chase whatever feels urgent in the moment. We work harder when stressed. We rest only when exhausted. We assume clarity will arrive later—once circumstances improve, responsibilities ease, or goals are met. We navigate the most consequential aspect of life without a *framework*.

The cost of this casualness is not theoretical. It shows up as chronic stress and quiet dissatisfaction. It manifests in strained relationships, and a persistent sense of *running but not arriving*. Later in life, it surfaces as regret. The regret is not about obvious mistakes. It is that so much effort was expended without clear direction.

Many people report the same pattern. They regret the lack of presence. They regret missing what mattered most. They realize they simply did not understand what actually supports a "good life."

The striking thing is not a lack of intelligence or effort. It is the absence of a reliable method. We lack a way to evaluate where we stand and what the next step should be.

This book addresses that gap.

It provides something basic and rare: a structured way to assess Well-Being and recognize progress as it unfolds.

Many excellent books explore ambition and ethics, contentment and inner freedom. What they rarely offer is *sequencing.* Readers are inspired, but left unsure how to move from where they are to where the book points. Once the book ends, the question quietly returns: "What now?"

This book takes a different approach. It treats Well-Being as a *system.* It can be understood structurally and developed progressively. It requires no leap of faith, nor adoption of a life that does not fit your reality.

The goal is ambitious because the problem is fundamental. We need to address Well-Being itself. We need orientation, not just insight. We need confidence in direction, not just encouragement.

Why a Map Matters

The methods of achievement are well known. We are taught how to study and work; how to optimize and advance. What is far less clear is direction.

We rarely pause to ask what kinds of effort actually compound into lasting Well-Being. We do not ask if our daily choices are strengthening us or draining us. We treat Well-Being as a "byproduct"—something that will arrive naturally once enough goals are met. Many discover, sometimes late, that success and Well-Being do not automatically align.

This book begins with that realization. It is not a rejection of ambition or responsibility. It is an invitation to re-orient. It asks three simple questions:

- What direction tends to support sustained Well-Being?
- What inner factors allow it to grow over time?
- How do we recognize whether we are moving toward it or away from it?

What follows is a clear way of seeing. The goal is to ensure that effort and relationships support our inner life, rather than compete with it.

The Geometry of Well-Being

Well-Being does not grow in a straight line. It unfolds in three dimensions, much like physical space expands from a point into volume.

Just as physical space is defined by **Length**, **Width**, and **Depth**, our inner life follows a similar geometry. We understand the stages in this book by how these three dimensions express themselves—and how they interact.

The Three Dimensions of Inner Experience

Before we can speak about maps or stages, we must ask a basic question: What is Well-Being actually made of?

At first glance, the answers seem obvious. We point to health and money, recognition and comfort, love and belonging. Yet experience quickly reveals a problem. There is no universal amount of wealth or praise that guarantees Well-Being. Two people can live under identical circumstances and experience life in profoundly different ways. One feels fulfilled; the other feels restless. One feels steady; the other feels fragile.

This tells us something essential. Well-Being is not determined by circumstances themselves, but by how those circumstances are experienced.

And experience, without exception, happens in one place. It happens in the mind.

We do not experience life directly. We experience interpretations. We interpret events and people; we interpret outcomes and ourselves. The world delivers stimuli, but the mind determines meaning. Our hands and eyes, ears and nervous system, function as *peripherals.* The mind is the *processor.* Life, as we live it, runs on this *inner operating system.*

This is why external factors cannot serve as the primary dimensions of Well-Being. Money and health, status and comfort, do not affect everyone in the same way. Their impact depends entirely on the condition of the inner system receiving them.

- A calm mind experiences scarcity differently than an anxious one.
- A stable inner life absorbs loss differently than a fragile one.

The same stimulus produces different lived realities. If Well-Being is to be understood structurally, it must be understood through the functioning of the mind itself.

When we look closely at lived experience, something striking appears. Despite infinite variations of personality or culture, the mind operates through three fundamental functions. They are so basic that we often overlook them. Yet they quietly shape every moment of our lives.

1. The mind *engages.* It plans and chooses; it desires and creates. This is the part of us that moves toward goals and takes responsibility. When this function is weak, life feels dull or burdensome. When it is strong, life feels alive and purposeful.

2. The mind *relates.* It defines what we include as "me" and what we treat as "other." It determines how we feel toward people and causes, communities and the world itself. Some experience life from a narrow center; others feel naturally connected beyond themselves. This function shapes care and empathy, conflict and belonging.

3. The mind *stabilizes.* It either remains steady under change, or it does not. This function determines whether peace depends on outcomes and approval, or whether it arises from within. When this function is weak, life feels fragile. When it is strong, challenges lose their power to destabilize us.

These three functions are not a new discovery. Across cultures and centuries, observers of human experience have independently arrived at similar distinctions—different names for the same underlying structure. The language varies. The functions do not.

Every lived experience—without exception—passes through these three capacities:

1. How we engage.
2. How we relate.
3. How stable we remain.

There is no fourth inner faculty through which experience occurs. Anything else we might name—purpose, meaning, joy, fear, motivation, or peace—emerges from some configuration of these three.

This is why Well-Being can be described through three dimensions—and why it does not need more.

- If engagement is absent, life feels *inert.*
- If relationship is narrow, life feels *isolating.*
- If inner stability is weak, life feels *fragile.*

And when all three are underdeveloped, Well-Being remains low regardless of external success. Conversely, when all three mature together, Well-Being becomes remarkably resilient—even under imperfect conditions.

This book does not claim that circumstances do not matter. It claims something more precise: circumstances matter only through the state of the inner system that receives them.

For this reason, the map that follows does not measure possessions, or achievements. It measures the inner dimensions through which all experience is filtered.

In the sections ahead, these three dimensions will be given clear geometric form. They will be named and explored. They will be applied consistently across every stage of the journey. They are not abstract concepts. They are lived realities you can observe in yourself.

Once you see them, you will begin to recognize them everywhere—in effort and exhaustion, in care and conflict, in calm and constraint. And from that point on, Well-Being will no longer feel mysterious. It will feel navigable.

An important clarification: The geometry you are about to see is a *structural lens*. It is not a *growth recipe*. Knowing the dimensions of a space does not tell us how a life actually moves through it. In practice, these dimensions rarely expand evenly. Increasing one without understanding its interaction with the others can create instability. This is why the journey through the stages is essential.

- **Length (The Extent of Engagement):** How fully do we participate in life? Some remain on the sidelines, trapped in inertia and indifference. Others engage actively. They create and serve. As engagement deepens, life begins to feel more purposeful. The movement here is from inaction to involvement, from avoidance to participation.

  Length reflects the proportion of your waking energy that is intentionally directed toward meaningful participation. It is not a measure of constant *busyness*. Rest, recovery, and reflection are part of a healthy system.

  To see your own Length, look at your energy across different roles.

  - **At work:** Do you do just enough to "survive," or do you bring a spirit of excellence to the task?
  - **In relationships:** Are you truly present? Or are you merely physically there while the mind is elsewhere?

  - **In health:** Do you drag yourself to the gym out of guilt, or do you engage with your body's vitality?
  - **In leisure:** Do you consume passively (scrolling)? Or do you create actively (learning, building, playing)?

  Length is the difference between *passing time* and *filling it.*

- **Width (The Scope of Identification):** How wide is our circle of concern? For many, effort begins and ends with the self. Then, gradually, it expands to family, community, society, and eventually to all beings. Each widening dissolves a little more of the ego's boundary, replacing possessiveness with care. The movement here is from self-centeredness to universality.

  To see your own Width, notice where your care hits a wall.

  - **The "Me" Wall:** Do I only act when there is a clear benefit for myself?
  - **The "Us" Wall:** I will do anything for my family, but do I view my neighbor's problem as "their issue"?
  - **The "Them" Wall:** Can I feel empathy for someone who disagrees with me, or does my care shut off when values clash?

  Width is not measured by how much you love those who love you. It is measured by how you treat those who can do nothing for you—especially when no one is watching.

- **Depth (The Source of Stability):** Where do we root our peace? When we depend on outcomes and recognition, our inner world rises and falls with circumstance. As maturity grows, stability shifts inward—toward clarity, conviction, and a ground that circumstances can no longer reach. The movement is specific: from dependence to inner freedom.

To see your own Depth, watch what happens when things shake.

- **When plans fail:** Does a missed deadline or a ruined vacation derail your entire week? Or can you adjust with a smile?
- **When validation vanishes:** If no one thanked you for your hard work today, would you still feel the work was worth doing?
- **When silence falls:** Can you sit alone for ten minutes without a phone? Or does the quiet make you anxious?

Depth is the distance between your Well-Being and the external world. It is the *buffer.* The deeper you go, the less you need the world to cooperate for you to be okay.

Understanding the Ranges

To see this geometry clearly, imagine each dimension expressed on a simple scale from 1 to 10. These ranges are not judgments. They are rough indicators of how constrained or expansive a dimension tends to be.

Length (Engagement):

Length has two dimensions: the *quality* of engagement—how fully present and intentional you are—and the *quantity* of engagement—the proportion of waking hours consciously directed toward meaningful participation. Both matter. High quality across a small proportion of hours is not full engagement. High quantity without quality is *mere busyness.*

- **1–3 (Inertia / Avoidance):** Doing the bare minimum. Wishing to be elsewhere. Energy withheld or misdirected.

- **4–6 (Compliance / Routine):** Doing what is required. Responsible, yet uninspired. Present in body, partially absent in spirit.
- **7–10 (Wholeheartedness):** Fully alive. Acting with care and craft. Bringing full presence to both the hours and the work within them.

A score of 5 or 6 reflects sustainable engagement within the natural limits of a human day—not partial commitment, but full quality across a realistic quantity. A score of 10 represents both maximum presence and the fullest possible proportion of waking hours directed with intention.

Width (Identification):

- **1–3 (Immediate Circle):** Concern is largely limited to oneself and close loved ones.
- **4–6 (Community):** Care extends to neighbors and colleagues, teams and familiar groups.
- **7–10 (Universality):** Compassion flows even toward strangers. It reaches those who oppose us.

Depth (Stability):

- **1–3 (Dependent):** Inner peace is determined by external outcomes.
- **4–6 (Resilient):** Setbacks can be absorbed, though they still leave a mark.
- **7–10 (Free):** Well-Being is rooted within. It remains relatively unshaken by gain or loss.

The Volume of Well-Being: A Thought Experiment

To better grasp the potential of this map, let us try a simple thought experiment. The numbers that follow are not measurements or judgments. They are only a way to make proportions visible.

A word on the formula itself.

The expression *Well-Being* = *Length* × *Width* × *Depth* is a model—and like all models, it is a simplification in service of clarity, not a claim to mathematical precision.

The choice of multiplication rather than addition is deliberate. The three dimensions do not merely contribute independently to Well-Being; they condition one another. A life with high engagement and wide concern but little inner stability is not simply a life with slightly less Well-Being—it is a life structurally vulnerable to collapse. When any dimension is very low, the whole suffers disproportionately. Multiplication captures that interdependence more faithfully than addition would.

The numbers assigned to each stage are not measurements. They are proportional illustrations—a way of making structural differences visible. The move from one stage to another represents a meaningful shift in configuration, not merely incremental improvement.

The skeptical reader is warmly invited to hold the formula lightly and test what matters: does the sequence ring true? Do the descriptions of these stages reflect something recognizable—in your own life, or in the lives of people you know well? That lived recognition is the only verification this framework requires or claims.

With that understanding in place, imagine the three dimensions expressed on the same scale.

- **Length (Engagement):** 1 represents inertia. 10 represents wholehearted participation in life.
- **Width (Identification):** 1 is self-absorption. 10 is a heart that naturally includes others.
- **Depth (Stability):** 1 is complete dependence on outcomes. 10 is an inner steadiness that does not rise and fall with circumstance.

If all three dimensions were fully expressed, the Volume of Well-Being would be:

$$\mathbf{10 \times 10 \times 10 = 1{,}000}$$

Now let us consider a familiar, responsible life.

Imagine someone who is doing "fine" by most standards. Let's call him Mark.

- **Length: 4.** Mark is engaged at work, but often tired or distracted, going through the motions more than he would like.
- **Width: 3.** He is a good, ethical person who loves his family deeply. He has a close circle of friends. His sustained concern rarely extends beyond them.
- **Depth: 3.** When things go well, he feels steady. When outcomes turn unfavorable, his peace is shaken.

Individually, these numbers feel reasonable. Together, they describe a responsible, decent life.

Look at the volume:

$$4 \times 3 \times 3 = 36$$

Even a life that feels "normal" may operate within a fraction of its potential.

What is encouraging is this: because these dimensions multiply, even small shifts can produce disproportionate gains.

If Mark becomes slightly more engaged (4 to 5); if he widens his care modestly (3 to 4); if he finds a bit more inner stability (3 to 4)—without changing his outer life dramatically—the volume expands quickly from 36 to:

$$5 \times 4 \times 4 = 80$$

He has not become a "monk." He has simply made small, human adjustments—yet the space within which he lives has more than doubled. That expansion is not abstract. It shows up in daily experience. His quality of life significantly improves:

- Recovery time shortens.
- Irritation dissipates faster.
- Setbacks no longer linger for days.
- Relationships feel warmer.
- Work feels less heavy.

This book is not asking you to reach a perfect 1,000. It is showing that even small, coordinated shifts can transform the lived texture of an ordinary, responsible life.

The Map of Stages

Using this geometry, the book traces a map of successive stages of Well-Being.

These stages are not moral rankings or philosophical ideals. They are ordered by *stability.* They measure the degree of freedom and internal sourcing a life can support. They are grounded in structure, observation, and lived testing. At each stage, you will be able to see—using the same geometry—why the next stage is more stable, and how it reduces the likelihood of regret.

Each stage represents a distinct configuration of the same three dimensions. What the map makes visible is that Well-Being does not improve merely by "trying harder." It improves when the right dimensions expand in the right relationship.

When engagement and identification expand, exposure increases. A larger life brings more experience—more opportunity, more connection, more responsibility. It also brings more uncertainty, disappointment, and complexity.

Without sufficient depth, expansion becomes unstable. A highly engaged and widely connected life without inner grounding is easily shaken. Success energizes it; setbacks destabilize it.

Depth is what allows expansion without fragility. Just as a tall structure requires a deeper foundation, a broad and active life requires an inner anchor that does not depend on outcomes.

This is why structural balance matters. Length and Width increase participation. Depth determines whether that participation remains steady under pressure.

This explains why so many people feel stuck despite trying hard. They invest heavily in one dimension while neglecting the others. Yet they do not realize that Well-Being does not increase linearly.

Without balance, effort stalls. With balance, it accelerates.

Seen through the geometry, the patterns are easy to recognize:

- They increase engagement without inner stability. The result is *burnout.*
- They widen care without inner stability. The result is *exhaustion.*
- They pursue stability without engagement. The result is *withdrawal.*

The stages show how the dimensions can mature together. When they do, effort compounds. As you move through the stages ahead, keep this image in mind: expansion without grounding leads to *strain;* expansion with depth leads to *strength.*

Throughout this journey, ambition does not disappear. It *evolves.* Ambition is the raw *kinetic force* of human life—the drive to move, to improve, to express, to become. What changes from stage to stage is not the energy itself, but the geometry that shapes it. In one stage it seeks personal advancement. In another, it submits to ethical guardrails. Later, it expands into contribution, stabilizes into balance, and eventually quiets into clarity. The energy remains. The structure transforms.

Why the Stages Matter

(And why the book does not end at geometry)

The geometry gives you the coordinates. The stages give you the path.

If this book were only a definition of three dimensions, it might be an interesting idea. It would not be a solution. It would not solve the real problem: How does a human life actually move from one configuration to another?

How do we do this without unrealistic leaps? How do we avoid personality-dependent advice? How do we do it without withdrawing from everyday responsibilities?

That is the purpose of the Map.

How Each Chapter Is Structured

This structure repeats across every stage, so you will always know where you are and what to expect.

- **The Lived Experience:** What the stage actually feels like from the inside. It describes the expansions that bring relief. It identifies the constraints that still create friction.
- **The Defining Traits:** The specific qualities required to enter and stabilize the stage.
- **The Geometry:** The dimensional score (Length × Width × Depth) and the structural logic behind the shape.
- **Tools to Maximize Well-Being:** Practical tools and protocols designed to expand dimensions without destabilizing the structure. These help you recognize progress through observable signals: *recovery time and clarity*; inner steadiness under pressure.
- **The Structural Limit:** An honest assessment of the maximum stability this stage can offer.
- **Closing Note and Invitation:** The specific signal that reveals the limits of the current stage. It is the friction that invites the next one.

This is not an ideal to accept on faith. It is built step by step. It uses the same geometry at every level. You will see for yourself why each transition works. You will see what actually changes as Well-Being deepens.

A Note on Stages and Personal Reality

Before moving forward, one clarification matters.

The stages presented in this book are not meant to catalogue every possible human state. That would be neither possible nor useful. Human lives are far more nuanced than any framework can fully capture. In reality, there may be as many inner configurations as there are individuals.

The stages you will encounter here are intentional selections. They are chosen to span the full arc of Well-Being—from deeply constrained states to extraordinarily stable ones. Together, they trace a coherent path. They make the movement from lower to higher Well-Being visible and understandable.

You may recognize yourself in several stages at once. You may not fully inhabit any single one. That is natural.

The purpose of these stages is twofold.

1. **Structural Assessment:** They help you assess Well-Being structurally. You will learn to see where constraint currently lies and why. Over time, this lens allows you to evaluate your own inner state without labels or comparison, without shame or self-judgment.
2. **Actionable Movement:** They help you identify the nearest upward movement available to you. Sometimes that movement is toward the next stage in the arc. At other times, it is about applying the principles of your current stage more fully. The goal is to make it stable and coherent. It is to make it *life-giving.*

The goal is not to rush forward. It is not to measure yourself against an abstract ideal. It is to understand what kind of growth is realistic and stabilizing right now.

It offers a map across the terrain. It provides tools that remain useful wherever you find yourself.

With that understanding, we can now turn to how to walk this journey.

How to Walk This Journey

A few things worth keeping in mind before you begin. These stages are not a test and not a label—most of us live several simultaneously, in different areas of life. The practices from later chapters can benefit anyone, even in early stages, so there is no need to wait. Treat the stages as *lenses* that orient your attention, not *ladders* that measure your worth. And let your own experience be the proof. Notice your *recovery time,* your clarity, the warmth in your relationships. Love and care are not stages. They are forces that strengthen any stage when present.

Orienting Questions

These questions are diagnostic, not prescriptive. Read them as an engineer would read instrument readings—for information, not judgment.

Circumstances & Agency

- Do I wait for conditions to improve? Or do I act to improve them?
- When upset, how quickly do I move from blame to responsibility?

Worth & Recognition

- How tightly is my mood tied to results or approval?
- If titles vanished, what in me would remain steady?

Emotions & Recovery

- Is there a hum of restlessness even when life seems "fine"?
- How quickly do I return to balance after a setback?

Relationships

- Do I keep a quiet ledger of giving versus receiving?
- When I help, is it mainly duty? Or is it joy?

Inner Compass

- Do I live by clear values under pressure?
- Where do words and actions align? Where do they break apart?

Meaning & Belonging

- What truly gives life value for me now?
- Where do I feel connected to something larger than myself?

You may recognize yourself in these prompts across many stages. That is natural. Let them open the journey. Do not let them narrow it.

We begin with the first stage: **Inertia.** It is not a flaw to be fixed. It is a common human experience. It is the natural starting point for understanding how movement becomes possible.

Chapter 1

The Geometry of Inertia

The Lived Experience of Inertia

Sarah is 28. Her friends describe her as ambitious. She talks easily about her plans—starting a side business, moving abroad, and learning design. Her social feeds are filled with motivational quotes. She follows people who seem to be building lives she admires.

But beneath her lively words, frustration quietly accumulates.

Weeks pass without action. Notebooks of ideas remain unopened. Online courses are bookmarked but not begun. Each success story she scrolls past briefly lifts her imagination. Then it lowers her confidence. "Why not me?" she wonders.

From the outside, Sarah appears fine. She speaks with energy. She smiles at gatherings. Because she sounds motivated, few realize that she feels stuck. Inside, her self-trust thins.

To protect herself from that discomfort, she begins to locate the cause outside herself. She shifts toward blaming circumstances. She points to the economy and office politics; she cites bad timing and unfair systems.

These explanations offer temporary relief. Yet, they postpone a harder question: what would it mean to act despite uncertainty?

Looking inward feels risky. It raises the fear that she might discover limitations she would rather not face. So she remains in *limbo*—wanting more and thinking more, but acting less.

The cost is subtle but real. Energy leaks into comparison instead of creation. Enthusiasm becomes *verbal* rather than *embodied.* Over time, Well-Being drains. It does not crash dramatically. It *leaks* persistently.

Reflection: The Mask and the Drain

Sarah does not lack desire. She lacks sustained engagement. Her confidence functions as a *mask.* It is not intentional; it is protective. It shields her from external judgment, but it also delays an honest reckoning with herself. And maintaining it has a cost—the energy spent sustaining the mask is energy unavailable for actual movement.

The inner costs accumulate quietly:

- Self-trust erodes each time intention is expressed without action.
- Responsibility shifts outward, reducing agency and self-respect.
- The gap widens between who she imagines becoming and what she practices daily.

The longer this gap persists, the more intimidating it feels to close. What began as hesitation slowly solidifies into inertia.

While Sarah represents a life largely shaped by inertia, most of us will recognize it selectively—in areas we quietly avoid, postpone, or treat as "tomorrow problems."

- You may be highly engaged at work, yet inert when it comes to your health.

- You may care deeply about family, yet rarely initiate contact.
- You may value reflection, yet never quite begin.

You may know what would help and still not act.

Inertia is not the absence of intelligence or intention. It is the absence of *motion in a specific direction* despite the capacity to move.

Seen this way, inertia is not a *verdict* on who you are. It is a *description* of where energy has not yet begun to flow. This pattern is not a personal failure. It is a predictable outcome of a constrained inner geometry.

Before looking at the traits of this configuration, one clarification matters. Sometimes a lack of movement arises from circumstances beyond one's control—illness, poverty, lack of safety or freedom. In such cases, Well-Being does not improve through effort alone. It requires care and support, and the restoration of basic stability. That is not the form of inertia explored here. This chapter looks at a configuration that appears even when external conditions are largely supportive—where opportunity exists, intelligence is present, desire is real, and yet movement hesitates.

The Defining Traits of Inertia

Inertia is maintained by three recurring patterns.

- **The *Waiting Mindset:*** motivation must arrive before action can begin. The individual waits for the right feeling or the right time. Because that *spark* rarely comes from outside, momentum never builds.
- **The *Comfort Bias:*** the pain of discipline feels greater than the pain of regret. Immediate relief wins over long-term gain.

- ***Low Agency:*** life feels like something happening to you rather than something you shape. When difficulties arise, the default is to identify an external cause. These factors may be real—but focusing on them surrenders the power to move.

What constrains Well-Being in this configuration is not a lack of ambition. It is a particular inner geometry.

The Geometry

Seen structurally, Sarah's experience is not mysterious. It reflects a configuration in which all three dimensions of Well-Being are constrained.

Length—Extent of Engagement (Score: 2)

Engagement is low. It is inconsistent. Action depends on mood; it does not rely on commitment. Motivation rises briefly. Then it dissolves.

Goals exist. Yet effort does not sustain itself long enough to generate momentum. Life is experienced more as a sequence of *reactions.* It is not actively shaped. Energy flows into imagining and explaining. It flows into comparison. It does not flow into deliberate action.

Width—Scope of Identification (Score: 1)

Identification narrows under pressure. It becomes *defensive.* Attention circles primarily around one's own frustrations and disappointments. It focuses on perceived disadvantages. This creates an inward pressure that feels isolating even in relationships.

Empathy for others exists. But it is easily overshadowed by resentment and fatigue. It is blocked by self-concern. The world feels like something happening to her rather than something she actively participates in. When engagement is inconsistent, identification struggles to express itself reliably.

Depth—Source of Stability (Score: 1)

At this stage, Depth has no independent source. Peace depends entirely on circumstances improving—on the world cooperating, the obstacle removing itself, the recognition arriving. This is not a flaw to be condemned. It is simply the starting condition: stability *borrowed* from the outside, waiting for a reason to begin from within.

Yet even here, something important remains intact. It is the awareness that "I am tired of feeling stuck." That moment of honest seeing is the first opening toward change.

Volume of Well-Being: 2 × 1 × 1 = 2

This number is not a judgment. It simply makes the constraint visible. It shows what happens when engagement and identification are limited. It shows the cost of low stability.

What This Geometry Explains

This configuration helps explain a common frustration: trying hard without moving forward.

Effort is present. It is *scattered.* Desire exists. It is not *embodied.* Stability is sought. Yet it is sought only through outcomes. The dimensions do not expand together. Therefore, energy *plateaus.* It does not *compound.*

Understanding this geometry shifts the question. It moves from "What is wrong with me?" to "What needs to expand first?"

The Structural Limit: Why Inertia Cannot Self-Resolve

Every stage of Well-Being has a ceiling—a point beyond which the structure cannot carry you further. For Inertia, that ceiling is low.

Even when circumstances improve or encouragement arrives; even when short bursts of motivation appear, the underlying geometry remains constrained.

Engagement *flickers.* It does not stabilize. Identification stays narrow. Inner stability remains conditional. This is why inspiration alone does not work here.

Inertia cannot be transcended through better information or stronger intention. It cannot be solved by waiting for clarity. As long as engagement depends on feeling ready, and responsibility remains externally oriented, Well-Being plateaus quickly.

Small improvements may occur. Yet, they do not compound. At its best, this configuration offers brief relief:

- A momentary lift from encouragement.
- Temporary hope from imagining change.
- Short-lived motivation sparked by comparison.

But these gains fade because the structure has not changed.

The defining limitation of this stage is specific: movement depends on *conditions* rather than *shaping* them. Until that relationship reverses, Well-Being remains fragile and inconsistent.

This is not a personal flaw. It is a structural fact. The moment sustained engagement begins, even in small doses, the geometry shifts. Length expands first. Momentum appears. Stability follows.

Inertia cannot be *perfected.* It can be *exited.*

Tools to Maximize Well-Being in Inertia

The aim here is not dramatic transformation. It is restored *agency.*

- **Face one truth.** Identify one area where circumstances are being blamed. Ask yourself: "What is one small action I can take despite them?" [This expands Length—it moves energy from explanation into action.]
- **Shrink the dream.** Large goals paralyze when engagement is low. Reduce them. Find a single 20-minute action you can complete today. [Small completions restore Depth—each finished action rebuilds self-trust.]
- **Notice the mask.** Pay attention to moments when you speak about change rather than act. Words are *signals.* They are not progress.
- **Build micro-courage.** Courage grows through repetition. It does not require intensity. Send one email. Enroll in one class. Make one appearance. [Each act of engagement, however small, begins shifting the geometry.]
- **Look inward gently.** This is not about judgment. It is about reclaiming *authorship* over your own movement.

Reflection Prompts

- What intention have I spoken about often, yet delayed acting on?
- After consuming success stories, do I feel energized or diminished?
- Where do I expect outcomes to come before engagement?
- Where has responsibility quietly shifted outward?
- What is one small action I can complete today without waiting to feel ready?

Simple Practices

- **The 20-Minute Rule:** Each time you talk about a goal, set a timer for 20 minutes. Take one concrete step. Draft or research. Practice. Action stabilizes intention.
- **The Ownership Swap:** When blame arises, write: "One thing I can do despite this." Even small ownership restores self-respect.

Closing Note and Invitation: Beginning the Ascent

This is the geometry of *misdirected energy:* strength turned inward as *explanation* rather than outward as *creation.*

The way forward does not require certainty or confidence. It does not need dramatic resolve. It begins with responsibility—taken *gently.* Taken *consistently.* Taken without *self-punishment.*

Each small act of engagement *extends* the length of participation. Each outward movement *widens* identification beyond the self. Each completed action *restores* a measure of inner stability.

You do not need to change your life overnight. Begin where you are. Use what you can.

Movement begins not with confidence, but with one honest step.

This is the invitation to Ambition.

Chapter 2

The Geometry of Ambition

The Lived Experience of Ambition

You have taken a decisive step beyond inertia. You no longer watch life pass by. You have begun shaping it—setting goals, taking responsibility, feeling the thrill of accomplishment. This is the awakening of high engagement.

In this stage, ambition takes its *self-advancing* form—energy organized primarily around personal achievement, security, and recognition. For many people, this stage is not a choice. It is a necessity. The world rewards ambition. In modern life, it often feels like the *price of admission*—the ticket to security and dignity, the cost of possibility.

Ambition brings powerful rewards and subtle costs. This chapter helps you celebrate its gifts while preparing you for the strains that often accompany them.

The Engine of Progress: The World's Debt to Ambition

Before exploring the inner geometry of the ambitious person, one thing deserves acknowledgment. Ambition is not merely a personal trait. It is a civilizational force. The modern city—its infrastructure, its institutions, its connectivity—is a monument to the ambition of millions. When channeled with care, this energy becomes a force for good. The scientist seeking a cure, the entrepreneur building an industry, the leader uniting a people—each carries its fingerprints. This chapter does not ask you to soften that energy. It asks you to *govern* it.

The Psychological Currency: Competence

Inertia feels like life is happening *to* you. Ambition feels like life is happening *through* you.

The deeper reward of ambition is not money or titles. It is *self-sufficiency.* It is the realization: "I can steer my own course."

One of the most valuable assets ambition provides is Competence. This is the quiet confidence that you can meet demands. You can shape outcomes.

Competence brings *security*—the trust that you can handle tomorrow. It brings *identity*—you are no longer someone's dependent but a contributor. And it brings *dignity*—the felt sense that your place in the world is earned.

Story: The First Paycheck

Kate still remembers her first real paycheck. It wasn't large. It was barely enough to cover rent and groceries.

But when she held it, she felt something priceless: proof of capability.

The slip of paper was more than money. It was evidence that she could generate value. She could make choices without asking. She could stand taller.

For someone who once lived in inertia, this difference is enormous. It is the shift from being a *pawn* on the chessboard to being a *player* with agency.

Reflection

- Do I remember a moment when I first felt capable in a new way?
- Was the dignity I felt proportional to the achievement? Or was it larger than the achievement?

Recognition, Belonging, and the Identity Boost

Ambition also brings recognition. It brings praise from a manager. It brings applause after a performance. It brings admiration from peers.

At its best, recognition affirms something human and tender: "I matter. My effort has value."

That validation motivates further growth. It strengthens identity. "Not only can I do this, but others see that I can."

Building Security: The Real Gifts of Ambition

Beyond confidence and recognition, ambition delivers tangible security:

- A dependable income.
- A stable home.

- Health routines that sustain energy.
- Skill growth that secures the future.

These are not small achievements. They transform life from "survival mode" into security.

That security, when done cleanly, can be a foundation for higher Well-Being.

Strategic Ambition: Cooperation Out of Self-Interest

The "Accidental Width" of Ambition

There is a beneficial side-effect within ambition.

Structurally, ambition often begins with narrow self-interest (Low Width). Yet to succeed, ambition is forced to build cooperation.

Ambition builds more than skyscrapers. It builds networks.

- Corporations form partnerships to expand markets.
- Nations enter treaties for security and growth.
- Competitors collaborate on standards that allow billions to connect.

What begins as pure self-interest often requires qualities we associate with ethics. It requires trust and reliability. It requires fairness and long-term thinking.

At the personal level:

- A professional mentors a junior colleague to strengthen reputation. **Result:** the mentee grows.

- A neighborhood leader organizes a drive for visibility. **Result:** The community benefits.
- A student volunteers to enhance a résumé. **Result:** Impact is created.

This is the "Accidental Width" of Ambition.

Even when the heart is not yet fully open, ambition weaves people together. It becomes a bridge between the isolation of inertia and the genuine compassion of later stages.

Reflection Pause

- Where has my self-interest created genuine benefit for others?
- Where have I cooperated not from love, but from necessity—and still seen good emerge?

The Fire That Powers This Stage

Ambition is fueled by energy. It is activity and projection. It is movement and momentum.

When this energy predominates:

- The mind buzzes with ideas.
- The calendar fills quickly.
- Rest seems less important than momentum.
- Silence feels unproductive.
- "More" feels natural.

This energy can build extraordinary things.

But fire must be contained.

Story: The Startup Founder

Edna left her corporate job to start her own company.

For months she ran on adrenaline. Twelve-hour days. Endless coffee. Constant pitches. Every "yes" sent her soaring.

But ambition is volatile fuel. Every "no" hit like a physical punch. Her inner state rose and fell like a rollercoaster. Rest felt like weakness. Silence felt unbearable.

The question is not whether ambition is good or bad. The question is whether it is governed.

The High-Wire Act: Why Ambition Feels Exhilarating—and Fragile

Ambition can feel like walking a tightrope above the crowd.

Each step forward brings applause. It brings admiration. It brings a rush of energy.

But beneath the thrill lies fragility. One wobble. One slip. It feels like everything could collapse.

Why?

Because ambition often comes with a hidden contract.

The Hidden Algorithm: The If-Then Contract

As ambition grows, a quiet error code slips into the operating system:

- If I achieve, then I am worthy.

- If I win, then I am safe.
- If I keep succeeding, then I matter.

It is rarely spoken. But it drives countless decisions.

This contract fuels high Length.

But structurally, it is a disaster. It *tethers* Depth to external variables. You cannot control them.

Story: The Missed Promotion

Lucas worked tirelessly. The promotion went to someone else.

He smiled outwardly but felt gutted inside.

For weeks he replayed conversations. He avoided colleagues.

The algorithm executed: "If Output = Failure, then Worth = Zero."

Reflection Pause

What is my own contract? Complete these lines:

- "If I succeed, then I am ..."
- "If I fail, then I am ..."
- "My worth depends on ..."

Read them back slowly. They are not wrong. They are simply your current contract. Naming them gives you power.

The Hedonic Treadmill

(The Feedback Loop That Keeps You Running)

1. Achievement triggers joy.
2. The mind *adapts.*
3. Joy fades.
4. Craving returns.

This is not moral failure. It is a biological feedback loop.

Jessica's Gilded Cage

Jessica is 35. Her life looks polished.

Her mornings begin with high-intensity workouts. Her days are deals and meetings. They are filled with deadlines. Her evenings are networking dinners. They are strategic visibility.

Her planner is a mosaic of colored blocks.

To colleagues, she is unstoppable.

But in the pauses—quiet hotel rooms after keynotes, the car ride after long days—Jessica feels a hollowness she cannot quite name.

Each milestone delivers a dopamine rush. The thrill fades quickly. No sooner has she reached one goal than her mind scans for the next.

The trophies gleam. They feel oddly silent.

She fears slowing down, because she has confused *motion* with *meaning.*

The very ambition that gave her freedom now feels like a "gilded cage."

The Defining Traits of Ambition: Productivity

Ambition is defined by one core shift: the ability to reliably convert effort into results.

This is *Productivity.* It is not constant activity. It is not exhaustion. It is effective output.

Work moves from *intention into execution.* Skills are applied. Progress becomes visible. Life begins to respond.

Productivity is not a single trait. It emerges when *discipline* stabilizes effort, *focus* prevents fragmentation, *determination* persists through friction, and *resilience* extracts lessons from failure—all working together to convert intention reliably into results.

The Geometry

Length—Extent of Engagement (Score: 6)

The person is in motion—charged, focused, industrious. Life feels like an open field of possibilities. Energy flows into goals. It flows into projects. It flows into performance. The rhythm is *expansion.* For many ambitious people, this means most waking hours are organized around performance, preparation, or progression—even leisure becomes *instrumental.*

Risk: The engine runs hot. "Do more" becomes a compulsion. Rest becomes rare.

Length at this stage is measured by both the proportion of waking hours consciously directed and the quality of immersion within them. A useful calibration: of sixteen waking hours, roughly ten hours of fully engaged, purposeful activity represents the human maximum—beyond which the system begins to deplete rather than compound. A score of 6 reflects this honest ceiling: not a failing, but the natural limit of effort-based engagement. The ambitious person often approaches or exceeds this threshold—and the risk that the description names is real. When the engine runs at maximum capacity without adequate recovery, Length becomes the very dimension that erodes the others. The ambition that drives engagement can, if unchecked, undermine the stability that makes engagement sustainable.

Width—Scope of Identification (Score: 3)

Identification expands beyond the isolated self, but remains boundary-based. The circle widens to include "mine": my family, my team, my company, my community, my nation. Energy is directed toward building and protecting this extended identity.

Others are valued strongly when they belong to the circle. Those outside it are viewed as competitors, threats, or abstractions.

Risk: Empathy is conditional. Care is intense but selective. Cooperation is strategic. The world is divided into *allies* and *adversaries.* Width grows—but not yet universally.

Depth—Source of Stability (Score: 2)

The source of Depth at this stage is *competence*—the earned confidence that comes from taking responsibility and producing results. This is real and valuable: it is more stable than the passivity of Inertia. But competence is still anchored to outcomes. Peace is only as steady as the *last result.* The foundation has been laid; it has not yet been insulated.

Risk: This is a high-aspect-ratio structure. It is a *skyscraper with a narrow base.* It looks impressive, but sways violently in the wind.

Volume of Well-Being: 6 × 3 × 2 = 36

This is the Geometry of Volatility.

It is an improvement over Inertia (2). Yet it is inherently unstable. High Length at shallow Depth does not require extreme hours to become destabilizing. Even sustained, ordinary levels of engagement feel heavy when inner stability depends entirely on outcomes.

The Structural Limit of Ambition:

Why Stability Cannot Be Maximized Here

Every stage of Well-Being has a ceiling—a point of diminishing returns. It is not because effort is lacking. It is because the underlying structure cannot support further stability. Ambition reaches that limit quickly.

Ambition produces high engagement, visible progress, and a strong sense of agency. But even when fully optimized, its geometry remains inherently unbalanced:

- Length expands rapidly.
- Width widens only instrumentally.
- Depth remains externally anchored.

This creates a structural ceiling on Well-Being.

The Best-Case Scenario: At its best, Ambition can remain high while becoming less volatile. This happens when Depth is partially decoupled from outcomes, and Width is widened enough to reduce isolation. The engine still runs fast, but it stops overheating.

However, no matter how skilled the ambitious person becomes, inner stability cannot fully decouple from outcomes at this stage.

- Wins still elevate the self.
- Losses still threaten it.
- Identity remains tied to performance.

This is why Ambition feels exhilarating and exhausting.

Even with the stabilizing nudges applied, peace remains conditional.

The mind is still running a hidden algorithm: "I am safe as long as I continue to succeed."

As long as this contract governs identity, Depth cannot deepen further. The structure may become more efficient. It cannot become fundamentally stable.

This is not a failure of ambition. It is its *design limit.*

A Special Note: The Financial Freedom Paradox

There is a specific dream that drives much of modern ambition: Financial Freedom.

The logic is compelling: "If I save enough money—and do it quickly—I can buy Well-Being."

The word *quickly* is rarely emphasized, but it is often implied. The urgency reshapes the geometry. Engagement intensifies. Moderation weakens. Time with loved ones is deferred. Health becomes negotiable. Depth becomes tethered entirely to future outcomes. The present becomes a *corridor* to escape rather than a place to *inhabit.*

The Truth

Money is a powerful tool for removing friction. It solves problems of survival. It solves problems of comfort and access. Poverty is a constraint that makes Well-Being harder to reach. To ignore this would be unrealistic.

Many people experience genuine Well-Being through wealth by consciously choosing travel, rest, learning, and entertainment. This is real engagement. It reflects a life in motion, not dullness or avoidance.

But the structure matters.

When accumulation becomes compressed into urgency, Length rises sharply while Depth thins. The system runs hot. Adrenaline replaces steadiness. Success feels necessary, not joyful. The goalpost shifts quietly—what once seemed "enough" becomes insufficient. What was meant to secure freedom begins to demand acceleration.

Even if financial targets are eventually reached, the nervous system does not immediately recalibrate. Years of urgency train the mind to scan for the next milestone. The engine does not know how to *idle.* The capacity to rest has quietly *atrophied.*

Money can remove friction in the external world. It cannot compensate for friction accumulated within.

The reason this form of Well-Being eventually plateaus is not because pleasure is wrong. It is that pleasure alone rarely widens identity (Width) or deepens stability (Depth). When novelty fades or conditions shift, the structure reveals its limits. Wealth removes certain external pressures—but if Depth has been neglected in the pursuit of "quickly," the inner volatility remains.

The Trap

Money builds the stage. It does not write the script.

Without inner growth, financial freedom often produces specific structural failures:

- **"Luxury Inertia" (Length collapses):** Freedom from work, but not freedom for purpose.
- **"Comfortable Isolation" (Width shrinks):** Privacy becomes separation.
- **"Asset Anxiety" (Depth remains external):** The anxiety of preserving replaces the anxiety of earning.

Verdict: Financial freedom is a *platform.* It is not a *destination.*

The geometry explains why. External friction can be reduced by wealth. Internal friction must be reduced by growth.

Tools to Maximize Well-Being in Ambition

How to Keep Ambition—Without Being Owned by It

The goal is not to weaken ambition. It is to prevent volatility from running your life.

We do that by strengthening the two underdeveloped dimensions:

- **Widen Width:** Ensure life isn't just "Me vs. World."
- **Deepen Depth:** Ensure peace isn't held hostage by outcomes.

Below are practices designed as structural reinforcements.

1) Internalize Metrics (Depth): The "Better Than Yesterday" Shift

What you do: When comparison arises, redirect the lens.

- Instead of "Did I beat them?" ask "Did I grow?"
- Write one line each evening: "One way I'm stronger than yesterday."

Why this works: Comparison ties your self-esteem to external variables (others' wins). Internal metrics tie self-respect to controllable variables (your growth). You control this. This is the first decoupling of Depth from outcome.

Watch for: The mind will try to turn even this into a scoreboard ("I *must* improve daily"). Keep it gentle. The aim is steadiness, not pressure.

2) Scheduled Stillness (Depth): Cooling the Engine

What you do: Block one hour weekly with no agenda.

- No productivity.
- No learning podcasts.
- No "self-improvement."
- Just space.

Why this works: Ambition creates an addiction to motion. Stillness triggers the withdrawal symptom: anxiety. If you stay, the system learns: "I can be okay without chasing." That learning is Depth.

Watch for: The first few times may feel pointless. They may feel uncomfortable. That discomfort is the practice working.

3) Test the If-Then Contract (Depth): Decouple Self from Scoreboard

What you do:

- After a win: "Am I truly more valuable today?"
- After a loss: "Has my worth truly diminished?"

Why this works: It exposes the hidden contract as a thought, not a truth. Depth grows when you stop treating outcomes as identity verdicts.

4) Expand "Accidental Width" (Width): One Unconditional Act

What you do: Once a week, do one act that has no strategic value.

- Anonymous kindness.
- Help someone you cannot benefit from.
- Contribute without being seen.

Why this works: Ambition trains the mind to ask: "What do I gain?" Unconditional action retrains the heart: "I can give without bargaining." That widens Width beyond utility.

5) Redefine Progress (Balance): Add One "Quiet Metric"

What you do: Pick one quality-based metric.

- Patience.
- Steadiness.
- Presence.

- Kindness.
- Integrity.

Track it lightly.

Why this works: Ambition overweights Length. Quiet metrics pull development into Width and Depth. They stabilize the structure.

Closing Note: The Limit of Momentum

Ambition lifts us out of Inertia. It builds capacity. It builds competence. It builds confidence. Its gift is *momentum.*

But momentum alone cannot create lasting stability. A life built only on ambition is structurally unbalanced. It is expansive, but not yet *grounded.*

The solution is not to abandon ambition. Nor is it to slow it prematurely. It is to widen the circle of identification and deepen the source of stability. Until the geometry broadens and the foundation strengthens, peace will remain tied to outcomes.

What comes next is not the end of ambition—it is its *refinement.* That is the next step in the geometry.

Chapter 3

The Geometry of Ethics

The Lived Experience of Ethics

In Ambition, ethics was often a *strategy:* cooperation helps me win. Here, ethics stops being a calculation and becomes *structural integrity.*

Virtue ethics is often misunderstood as a list of rules to follow to be "good." From a geometric perspective, it is something far more practical: it is the *load-bearing framework* of a stable mind. Practiced sincerely, ethics deepens Well-Being not by adding "more," but by aligning life with what is true, non-harming, and balanced.

For the first time in this journey, Well-Being no longer entirely depends on outcomes. Earlier stages tethered peace to achievement, recognition, or security. Here, whether circumstances are favorable or harsh, their grip loosens. This is the first real step toward *less-conditional* Well-Being.

The Defining Traits of Ethics

Virtue ethics can feel abstract until we see how it works in daily life. A simple way to understand it is through three guiding traits—the "Three Anchors" that stabilize the mind:

- **Truthfulness:** The *alignment of the Intellect.* Living in alignment with reality reduces mental friction.
- **Non-injury:** The *alignment of the Heart.* Relating with restraint stabilizes the emotional climate.
- **Moderation:** The *alignment of the Body.* Using resources with balance prevents system burnout.

Together, these three create an integrated foundation: intellect aligned, emotions softened, body balanced.

PART 1: Alignment with Truth

The Intellect's Compass

Truthfulness is more than "not lying"—something I did not fully understand for years. It is the *alignment of our intellect with reality.* It means not distorting facts to make ourselves look better, not hiding from inconvenient truths, and not living by double standards. When the intellect is anchored in truth, life feels less *scattered.* Decisions are simpler. Memory is lighter.

Anxiety thrives in dishonesty. Why? Because lies must be remembered, reputations maintained, masks held up. This requires constant processing power. Truth, by contrast, *simplifies.* It may sting in the moment, but it clears the fog.

Story: The Inflated Résumé

Rohit had his dream interview lined up. A mentor suggested "polishing" his résumé—exaggerating a project's scope, inflating his leadership role. "Everyone does it," the mentor said. Rohit followed the advice. The interview went well—until the panel probed deeper. His vague answers betrayed him, and he left deflated. Months later, after much soul-searching, he applied again—this time with a clean résumé. He was nervous, but strangely calm. He did not get the job immediately, but he walked out without the knot in his stomach. "At least I know I was real" he told himself. That *inner steadiness* became its own strength.

Why Truthfulness Promotes Well-Being

- **Reduces System Friction:** Dishonesty creates friction between thought and action. Living truthfully restores *integrity.*
- **Strengthens relationships:** Trust is fragile; one small crack can shatter it. Truth builds the foundation for lasting bonds.
- **Stabilizes Self-Respect:** When you live truthfully, you do not have to rehearse or fear exposure. Self-esteem becomes *quieter,* but more resilient.
- **Medicinal Effect:** Many people notice a simple effect: when they stop distorting reality—even in small ways—tension drops. The mind stops rehearsing, defending, and managing a story.

When Truth Is Tested

Untruths often slip in not because we are malicious, but because we are afraid:

- Fear of losing reputation.
- Fear of disappointing others.
- Fear of facing ourselves.

That is why truthfulness requires courage. It is not about brutal honesty that wounds others; it is about gentle alignment—finding ways to be truthful without being harsh, and to face facts without denial.

Everyday Shortcuts: The Hidden Cost

Most of us do not commit billion-dollar frauds. But we face truth tests in smaller ways—jumping a queue, returning a used product, exaggerating on a résumé. Each act can feel harmless. "Everyone does it." Yet even when dishonesty works, it carries hidden costs: the anxiety of exposure, a *fragmented identity* split between who you are and the story you tell, and a quietly corroded self-respect. The mind grows restless, always calculating: "Will I be caught? What excuse will I give?" What starts as small shortcuts creates a climate—internal and external—where suspicion, stress, and resentment flourish.

The reward of truthfulness is more than just being "a good person." It is the inner freedom of not carrying *double lives,* the outer strength of being trusted, and the societal gain of smoother cooperation.

A Different Kind of Strength

It takes courage to stay truthful in a world that often rewards shortcuts. The strength of it is not in its immediate payoff; it is in the long-term solidity it creates.

- A business built on truth may grow slower, but its foundations endure.
- A life lived truthfully may miss some shortcuts, but it gains freedom from masks, from fear and from the exhausting work of pretending.

PART 2: The Power of Non-Injury

The Heart's Compass

Non-Injury is the refusal to cause unnecessary harm—in thought, word, or deed.

It is an *orientation:* "I will not harm, because harming diminishes me as much as it diminishes you."

What Non-Injury Does Internally

Non-Injury may look like a gift to others, but its deepest reward is felt by the one who practices it.

- It quiets anger. Choosing not to lash out shifts energy from *agitation* to *composure.*
- It softens fear. When you live gently, you stop creating enemies in your imagination.
- It nurtures compassion. Resisting harm naturally grows empathy—you see more clearly what others feel.

Non-Injury in Daily Life

Non-Injury is not only for saints and freedom fighters. It shows up in choices as small as these:

- Holding back a harsh word when you know it would wound.
- Listening fully before replying, even in disagreement.
- Choosing patience with a child or elder when irritation tempts you.

Each choice plants a seed of Well-Being within and around you.

Story: The Gentle Manager

Rachel managed a team under intense pressure. Deadlines loomed, mistakes happened, and tempers flared. She had every reason to scold. But she chose another path. She corrected firmly but without humiliation. She asked questions instead of assigning blame. Months later, her team not only met targets but described her as the safest boss they had ever had. Her calm had become their calm. Rachel discovered that leading without harm did not weaken results—it strengthened them.

Non-Injury Is Often Confused With...

- Passivity—but non-injury is *active restraint,* not inaction.
- Weakness—but it requires strength to absorb tension without returning it.
- Silence—but it allows firm truth spoken without injury.

When practiced, non-injury brings:

- Peace in relationships. People feel safe, lowering defenses and opening space for trust.
- Resilience in conflict. Without aggression as fuel, disputes lose their sharpest edges.
- Inner harmony. You stop carrying the *poison* of your own harshness.

When Harm Becomes Habit

To appreciate non-injury fully, notice what happens when its opposite takes root.

- Anger drains energy, leaving exhaustion behind.
- Harshness corrodes trust.
- Resentment lingers long after the words are spoken.

PART 3: Moderation as Balance

The Body's Compass

Every system has limits. When one drive expands without restraint—ambition without rest, pleasure without pause, accumulation without reflection—the structure begins to tilt. Moderation is not about shrinking life; it is about distributing energy wisely. It preserves rhythm. It protects renewal. Without moderation, engagement burns hot and then collapses. With moderation, energy *compounds* because it is allowed to recover.

Moderation is therefore not a denial of desire. It is the intelligent *pacing* of it.

Story: The Late-Night Scroller

Natasha worked hard, but her evenings often dissolved into scrolling social media. It felt like relaxation. But hours slipped away, sleep suffered, and mornings grew foggy. She was not lazy—she was caught in excess. One evening, she paused. Instead of scrolling, she read for twenty minutes. The difference was striking. She slept better and woke refreshed. Moderation did not require giving up her phone. It required drawing a boundary. That small shift gave her back clarity.

Story: Terry and the "Never Enough" Spiral

Terry is 39, a senior manager with a good income. Yet her peace is constantly shaken by comparison. A colleague buys a larger home, and she feels her apartment is small. Her social feed scrolls like a ledger of what she lacks. The irony is that she already has more security than most—but desire, unmoderated, blinds her to it. When she begins a simple gratitude practice, her lens shifts. She sees her privileges. The craving quiets. Moderation did not shrink her life; it let her finally live it.

Moderation stabilizes Length by making engagement sustainable. Energy stops leaking into excess, and your days regain rhythm—effort with recovery, ambition with balance.

Why Ethics Raises Well-Being Even When Life Doesn't Get Easier

A mind aligned with truth, a heart aligned with non-injury, and a body aligned with moderation, form the ethical foundation of Well-Being—one that multiplies peace, resilience, and dignity at every step.

These anchors also strengthen the geometry directly: truth reduces inner friction (Depth), non-injury widens the field of care (Width), and moderation stabilizes sustainable effort (Length).

The Geometry

Length—Extent of Engagement (Score: 5)

Engagement drops deliberately. The pace is no longer frantic. There is *rhythm* rather than *rush.*

This is not a retreat. In Ambition, the engine ran at maximum capacity—and that risk was real. Here, moderation installs a *governor.* The system slows not because energy has been lost, but because energy is now being managed. Effort flows in a sustainable cycle: engagement, then recovery, then engagement again. The person works with the same intention as before, but without the compulsion to fill every available hour.

The drop from 6 to 5 is *structural intelligence,* not diminishment. A system running at *sustainable capacity compounds* over time. A system running at *maximum capacity depletes.*

Width—Scope of Identification (Score: 4)

The field of care widens beyond "me" and "mine." In Ambition, others were valued when they belonged to the circle—and viewed as competitors or abstractions when they did not. Here, that boundary softens.

Truthfulness in the intellect naturally reduces the tendency to distort others—to see them as threats, rivals, or tools. Non-injury in the heart restrains the impulse to wound, which quietly expands the range of people the person can remain open toward. Care is no longer purely conditional on belonging. It extends, more steadily, to those outside the immediate circle—colleagues, neighbors, people encountered in passing—not yet universally, but with genuine warmth rather than strategic calculation.

Width here is not yet wide. But it has changed its basis—from protection of what is *mine* to respect for what is *human.*

Depth—Source of Stability (Score: 4)

Ethics deepens Depth through two distinct mechanisms, which is why the gain here is larger than at any single stage. The first is *integrity:* when action is aligned with values, the mind carries less friction—no residue of self-betrayal, no quiet guilt, no energy spent managing contradiction. Even when outcomes disappoint, self-respect holds. The second is the inner space created by *non-harm* and *moderation:* when the tendency to wound others is restrained and appetite is kept proportionate, the mind and body become less burdened—there is less turbulence to manage, less reactivity to contain. Integrity raises the *floor.* Space lowers the *noise.* Together, they produce stability that earlier stages could not reach.

The Volume of Well-Being: 5 × 4 × 4 = 80

The Geometric Insight: Structure vs. Effort

The jump in volume from Ambition (6 × 3 × 2 = 36) to Ethics (5 × 4 × 4 = 80) is striking. But the deeper insight is not simply the increase in total effort. It is the effect of structural balance.

To illustrate this more clearly, let us equalize the raw scores (the "Total Input").

In its lived form, Ambition has a total input of 11 (6 + 3 + 2). Ethics has a total input of 13 (5 + 4 + 4). What happens if we increase Ambition's Engagement score from 6 to 8 to raise its total input to match Ethics at 13?

- Ambition (adjusted): 8 + 3 + 2 = 13 | Volume: 8 × 3 × 2 = 48
- Ethics: 5 + 4 + 4 = 13 | Volume: 5 × 4 × 4 = 80

Even with identical total input (13), Ethics still produces a volume of 80 which is substantially higher than Ambition's 48.

Why?

Because Well-Being does not scale linearly with effort. It scales structurally.

When effort is distributed more evenly across engagement, identification, and inner stability, the system becomes dramatically more efficient. The same amount of human energy produces far greater peace.

This is the hidden gift of Ethics.

An ethical life feels calmer and more peaceful at rest. It is not because life has become easier, but because the inner structure is more balanced. Energy is no longer stretched thin along a single axis. The system holds itself.

The Structural Limit of Ethics

Ethics is the first stage where Well-Being becomes meaningfully less dependent on outcomes.

But ethics has a structural ceiling.

Even when these principles are sincerely practiced, the stage can still feel quietly incomplete for one main reason:

Ethics improves the inner compass but does not automatically expand the field of play.

- Width expands in intention (fairness, care, restraint), but it may not expand in lived experience unless it expresses itself through action.
- Length becomes cleaner and more sustainable, but it can also become cautious: fewer risks taken, fewer impulses followed, fewer "big wins" pursued.
- Depth stabilizes, but it may stabilize as *self-contained peace* rather than *overflowing joy*.

The ethical person often reaches a plateau that sounds like this:

"I feel more grounded and less conflicted... but life also feels contained. I'm not hurting myself or others—but I'm not yet fully alive in giving."

This isn't a flaw. It's a structural fact.

Ethics can produce *poise*—but *poise* alone does not produce *fullness.*

Tools to Achieve Maximum Well-Being in Ethics

Gentle Nudges Toward Truthfulness

- Start small. Pick one area where you habitually exaggerate (social media, excuses). Practice simple, clean truth there.
- Truth check-ins. At day's end, ask: "Did I imply anything today that was not fully real?"
- Truth in silence. Sometimes the challenge is not lying, but avoiding. Practice saying, "I do not know" or "I cannot commit" instead of over-promising.
- Truth with kindness. Truth does not need cruelty. Aim for clarity wrapped in care.
- Personal alignment. Beyond words, ask: "Are my daily actions in line with what I claim to value?" If not, choose one adjustment this week.

Reflection Prompts for Truthfulness

- Where do I most often bend or avoid the truth—to impress, to protect, or to escape?
- What does it feel like in my body when I distort truth versus when I stay aligned?

- If my worth did not depend on approval or image, what truths would I live more openly?
- When have I experienced relief or dignity simply from being honest, even at a cost?

Gentle Nudges for Practicing Non-Injury

- Pause before the tongue burns. When anger flares, breathe once. Ask: "Will these words heal, or will they scar?"
- Choose compassion over correction. When someone errs, ask if gentleness will teach better than harshness. Often, it does.
- Redirect energy. Channel frustration into movement (a walk, a stretch) before responding.

Reflection Prompts for Non-Injury

- What is one memory where words hurt me more deeply than any physical wound?
- When was the last time my words or actions unintentionally hurt someone I care about?
- What would it feel like to live in such a way that people feel lighter, not heavier, after meeting me?
- Can I recall a moment when I chose restraint and it preserved a relationship?

Gentle Nudges for Moderation

- Define *enough.* Write down what "enough" looks like for you in money, possessions, or entertainment. Use it as a gentle guardrail.

- Balance indulgence with repair. Enjoy the dessert—but also the walk. Watch the movie—but also the sleep.
- Spot *diminishing returns.* Notice when pleasure plateaus. The second piece of cake rarely tastes as good as the first. Stop there.

Reflection Prompts for Moderation

- Where in my life do I regularly slip into excess and how does it affect my energy?
- Where do I feel the pull toward more—and what is the cost of following it?

Common Traps

Virtue ethics does not instantly make life easy. At first, it often feels harder. You are turning inward for stability, but the world is not playing by the same rules.

Typical friction points include:

- **Anger at the "Unfair Win":** When corner-cutters get rewarded, resentment rises. "Is the world laughing at me?"
- **Judgment:** Seeing clearly can slide into looking down on others. Judgment hardens the heart and leaves you lonely.
- **Martyr Energy:** Doing the "right thing" while secretly hoping someone will notice. When they don't, bitterness grows.
- **Perfectionism:** Ethics becomes a performance scorecard. One slip, and you feel like a fraud.
- **Systemic Fatigue:** Unjust teams or policies wear you down. Ethical living can feel like swimming upstream.

Gentle Guardrails While Your Roots Grow

- Choose your company. Like a sapling shielded from harsh wind, spend time with people who value truth and balance.
- Name it, don't nourish it. When resentment or envy shows up, label it softly: resentment... envy... breathe. Labeling loosens the emotion's grip.
- Practice "clean nos." Compassion without collusion: say no to unethical asks without contempt. One sentence, calm tone, no sermon.
- Small joys, daily. Ethical steadiness needs energy. Sleep, walks, and friendship are not luxuries; they are fuel.
- Serve quietly. Anonymous good acts starve the ego of applause and feed the heart with quiet warmth.

Questions

- **Will living ethically mean falling behind?**

Not necessarily—Chapter 2 showed that trust compounds over time, and the short race is rarely the one that matters.

- **What if others take advantage of honesty?**

The risk is real, but a life built on deception corrodes from within. Your peace remains intact when you act from alignment, regardless of how others behave.

- **Does ethics mean surrendering ambition?**

No—ambition is energy; ethics is the *compass.* Together they produce focused effort without the restlessness of endless craving. And moderation is not mediocrity—it is the condition under which all other dimensions can compound rather than deplete.

Closing Note and Invitation: From Integrity to Overflow

The gift of Ethics is inner integrity. It is the relief of no longer living at war with yourself. Truth reduces mental friction. Non-harm softens relationships. Moderation restores balance. You become steadier, cleaner, and harder to shake.

But this stage also reveals something quietly important: a good life is not only the absence of regret—it is the presence of giving.

When your inner structure becomes stable, something natural begins to happen: it wants to *overflow.*

The next chapter explores that overflow—Contribution—where engagement rises again, not from craving or competition, but from the quiet strength and widened heart that Ethics has built.

Chapter 4

The Geometry of Contribution

The Lived Experience of Contribution: From Alignment to Overflow

When inner life aligns—truth in the mind, compassion in the heart—steadiness does something extraordinary: it *overflows.*

This chapter is about that overflow. Contributive Well-Being is what happens when inner coherence turns outward as care, mentorship, and service. You do not stop being ambitious; you start letting your effort benefit more than yourself. It is not a moral performance. It is a *Natural Expansion.*

Think of a candle. In Ethical Well-Being (Chapter 3), the candle is whole and well-crafted. In Contributive Well-Being, it is *lit.* The point was never only to be well-crafted; it was to give light, drawing from a steady inner source.

Story: The Teacher's Light

A retired schoolteacher once said, "The greatest joy of my career was not the awards; it was running into former students who told me, 'You changed my life.' The candle of my work still burns in them."

From "Me" to "We": The Structural Shift

Ambitious Well-Being is a journey of the *Me*—my goals, my security. Ethical Well-Being makes the *Me* virtuous. Contributive Well-Being expands the *Me* to include the W*e*. This expansion shows up geometrically as greater Width and Length, before Depth has fully caught up.

The journey from Ambition to Contribution is a major expansion of consciousness. It is the shift from the narrow confines of a self-centered ego to an expanded identity.

- The ambitious person builds a network to get ahead.
- The contributive person builds a network to lift others.

This expansion is not just a moral choice; it is a *psychological evolution.* The individual's identity, once tied to personal achievements, now encompasses family, community, and society. The "I" is still present, but it has expanded its borders.

It is the shift when a person realizes that their own happiness is not separate from the happiness of those around them. This is the stage where a person voluntarily and enthusiastically dedicates themselves to a cause greater than self-interest. They find fulfillment in mentoring a young professional, in volunteering for a local charity, or in using their skills to solve a social problem.

Reflection Prompts:

- Who in my life has served me in ways that went beyond themselves?
- In what small ways have I already expanded from "me" to "we"?

The Unseen Rewards of Giving

The journey of Contributive Well-Being marks a significant transition, and the rewards that accompany it are unlike anything you have experienced before. They are the unseen rewards—the deep, intrinsic fulfillment that comes not from what you get, but from what you give. In a world that teaches us to value what we can acquire, this is a radical and liberating truth. The rewards here are not measured in dollars or praise, but in a quieter peace that doesn't depend as much on outcomes.

The transactional nature of the ambitious stage creates a constant sense of scarcity. "Getting mode" feels like filling a bucket that is never full; giving can flip you into "source mode"—a quieter sense of abundance. Over time, it subtly shifts how the mind relates to effort and reward.

Many people notice something surprisingly tangible: giving often lowers stress and lifts mood, which makes the next act of giving easier. This creates a positive feedback loop: the more you give, the better you feel—and the more you want to give. This is why a truly generous person often appears to be radiating a quiet joy. They are living proof that a life built only on getting stays *hungry,* while a life that gives begins to feel *whole.*

Exercise: A Day of Giving

- Tomorrow, choose one deliberate act of giving (time, attention, kindness).
- Do it without announcing it.
- At the end of the day, write: "Did this lighten me or weigh me down?"

If it lightened you, that is the signal: the act itself contains its own reward.

Applying This to Real Life: Returning to Jessica

Remember Jessica from Chapter 2? She was the high-achiever living in the "gilded cage", where every promotion brought a momentary thrill followed by a hollow restlessness. She was trapped in "getting mode"—trying to fill an inner void with outer wins.

She doesn't need another achievement. She needs contribution.

If Jessica dedicates just one hour a week to a context other than herself—mentoring, creating something useful, showing up for family with steadiness, using her professional skill for someone else's progress, serving those with difficult basic needs—her perspective begins to shift.

In the face of real struggle of others, her own corporate anxieties about deadlines and titles suddenly look small. She moves from *getting* to *giving,* and for the first time, her worth is not tied to winning, but to sharing. This awakens gratitude for the privileges she often overlooks.

That gratitude does what success never could: it begins to calm her nerves. The frantic hum of "more, more, more" quiets down, replaced by the warmth of being *enough.* By stepping out of her cage to help another, she inadvertently frees herself.

The Quiet Hand that Gives

Real contribution is rarely loud in the ways we expect. It does not announce itself or seek applause; it simply responds to life's need.

There are countless unseen acts of service that sustain the world—the neighbor who shares a meal, the stranger who stops to help, the friend who lends without expecting anything in return. My father was one such quiet giver. He did not have wealth to spare, yet his heart overflowed with generosity.

He once met a father struggling to pay his child's college fees—a bright boy who risked losing his chance at education. My father, who had little himself, took a personal loan and gave it to him. That boy went on to graduate and later study abroad. A single, silent act of kindness changed the course of another's life.

To him, helping was never a calculation; it was *reflex*—a natural flowering of compassion. True contribution often arises that way: not from surplus, but from empathy. It comes not from the wallet but from the heart's readiness to share.

Ethical living builds the vessel; love, over time, fills it. When gratitude matures into this kind of sweetness, giving stops being effort—it becomes an *expression.* The world, in truth, rests more on such invisible kindness than on any grand design.

The Shadow Side: The Silent Ledger

The journey of Contributive Well-Being is both beautiful and bittersweet. Giving brings a deep joy that ambition never could, yet it also carries an undercurrent of pain. This is because the ego, though expanded from "me" to "we," still lingers. Service may appear selfless on the outside but on the inside, the ego often keeps a subtle *score*. This inner bookkeeping is the "Silent Ledger."

The mind records every sacrifice: the chores done, the hours given, the emotional support offered. Then it scans outward, comparing—"What have they done in return?" When the account feels unbalanced, disappointment sets in. The thought arises: "I do more for them than they do for me." With that thought, the joy of giving begins to *sour*. At this stage, *conditionality* is not a flaw—it is a structural limit.

One of the clearest ways this shadow shows up is in everyday life. Take Anita, for example.

Mini-Story: The Forgotten Birthday

Anita spent hours planning her friend's surprise party, only to have her own birthday pass unnoticed months later. The quiet hurt was not about the cake—it was about feeling unseen. Her giving carried an unspoken ledger.

For many, this is most acute in family life or caregiving roles. Love flows freely, yet when gratitude is absent, resentment quietly grows. Acts meant to bring closeness can ironically create distance. The giver feels "unseen," even "used," and the peace once drawn from service begins to feel fragile. The ego, still craving recognition, whispers: "I gave, but where is my return?"

Gentle Nudge

"When I give, do I keep a silent score? If so, can I notice it without judgment—just as a signal of where my ego still clings?"

Living In "No-Man's Land"

You are giving more than ever, yet there is still an undercurrent of conditionality. When thanks or acknowledgment do not come, the disappointment cuts sharply because so much of yourself was invested. In these moments, you find yourself in a transitional no-man's-land.

- You cannot go back to Ambition's narrow self-interest (you know too much now).
- But you have not yet reached the freer, less-conditional space of selfless giving.

This tension is not failure; it is a *Signal of Growth*. It reveals the limit of the ego. This is what an expanded but imbalanced geometry feels like from the inside.

Ledger Reset (90 Seconds)

1. **Name it:** "I am keeping score."
2. **Re-anchor:** "My reason for giving is alignment, not applause."
3. **Re-choose:** Either give freely or set a clear boundary—and release the tally.

Defining Traits for Contribution

Contribution is defined by one core shift:

The ability to direct sustained effort toward the Well-Being of others—without immediate personal gain as the primary motive.

This is generative engagement.

Unlike ambition (which converts effort into results), contribution converts alignment into impact. Energy no longer terminates at the self; it flows outward.

Generative engagement is not a single virtue. It emerges when several enabling traits work together.

The Enabling Traits of Contribution

- **Care Orientation:** The genuine concern for others' Well-Being—not as an obligation, but as a natural extension of identity.
- **Expanded Identity:** The sense that "my life" includes family, mentees, teams, or community. The self has widened beyond the individual boundary.
- **Service Willingness:** The readiness to offer time, effort, or skill even when it costs comfort, convenience, or recognition.
- **Relational Attunement:** Sensitivity to what others actually need (not just what you want to give). This prevents performative or misdirected service.
- **Boundary Awareness (Early Form):** An emerging—but still imperfect—ability to sense when giving is becoming depleting, even if limits are not yet cleanly enforced.

Together, these traits push Length and Width forward rapidly, while Depth grows—but remains partially dependent on feedback, gratitude, or visible impact.

The Geometry

Length—Extent of Engagement (Score: 6)

Engagement rises again to levels seen in Ambition—but the quality of that engagement has changed.

In Ethics, Length was intentionally moderated. We slowed the system down to install structural integrity: truth in the mind, non-harm in the heart, balance in the body. That restraint was necessary. It ensured that energy would no longer be reckless or corrosive.

Once that integrity is in place, something important happens: higher engagement becomes safe again.

In Contribution, the *governor* is no longer suppressing energy—it is guiding it. Effort accelerates not from fear, competition, or proving, but from *overflow.* The engine runs fast again, but the fuel has changed. Engagement is now animated by *care* rather than *anxiety.*

This is why Length legitimately returns to a high value. The system is active, productive, and outwardly engaged—without reverting to volatility.

Width—Scope of Identification (Score: 5)

Width expands modestly but meaningfully beyond Ethics.

Ethics widened the heart through *respect*—recognizing others as ends, not means. Contribution widens it further through *joy.*

When care is translated into action, something experiential occurs: giving feels good. This is not sentimental; it is structural. The mind receives direct evidence that opening outward does not lead to loss—it leads to vitality. That positive feedback lowers defensive boundaries.

As a result, the perimeter of care expands beyond principle into lived connection: colleagues, mentees, teams, family, community. The heart opens with greater confidence, not merely obligation.

Yet this expansion is still *selective.* Care tends to flow toward people, causes, or contexts that resonate with identity and values. The ego still defines the boundary—wider than "me," but not yet universal.

This is why Width increases, but does not yet leap.

Depth—Source of Stability (Score: 5)

Depth deepens further—but carefully, and for specific reasons.

This increase is not a jump; it is an addition.

The new source of Depth at this stage is *meaning*—specifically, the experience that one's effort matters beyond oneself. This form of stability is less fragile than outcome-dependence, because the sense of purpose does not vanish when a single project fails. It does, however, still depend on a response from the world: appreciation, visible impact, reciprocity. When those are absent, the layer *wobbles.* Depth has grown, but its outermost layer remains *conditionally anchored.*

That conditionality matters. It explains both the increase in Depth—and its limit.

Structural Summary

The resulting geometry is expansive and powerful:

- Length is high and purposeful.
- Width is warm and connected.
- Depth is layered, but not yet unshakable.

The overall volume of Well-Being increases significantly:

Ambition emphasized speed, with limited structural support. Ethics prioritized balance, doubling stability at the cost of pace. Contribution combines high engagement with widened care and added meaning—the structure grows not by pushing harder on one axis, but by distributing effort more intelligently across all three.

The Volume of Well-Being: 6 × 5 × 5 = 150

The Structural Limit of Contribution

The progression is clear. We have grown significantly.

Best stability this stage can enable (when its nudges are applied): Length stays high and purposeful, Width expands with warmth, and Depth becomes less dependent on gratitude—so giving feels light, not depleting.

But the limit remains. Both Width and Depth are still *tethered* to response—to appreciation, visible impact, and reciprocity. When those are present, the structure holds beautifully. When they are absent for long, the joy of giving begins to thin. The ceiling of this stage is not a failure of generosity. It is the natural boundary of an identity that has expanded, but not yet *dissolved its need for return.* To go further, giving must become genuinely *unconditional*—which requires a stability that no longer depends on the world's response at all.

Tools to Maximize Well-Being in Contribution

How to stay contributive without burning out

To stay contributive without becoming depleted, use this five-part pacing tool. It is not a moral scoreboard—it is a practical guide to keep your giving light and sustainable.

1) **Compass**—"Why am I giving?"

Ask: "What is my reason?"

If it is love, care, or a genuine sense of purpose, you can give freely—but not blindly. Let your reason keep you steady when outcomes vary.

2) **Capacity**—"Can I afford this?"

Ask: "Do I have surplus here—or am I already strained?"

Check quickly: time, energy, money, attention. If saying "yes" will create resentment, risk, or depletion, scale the gift or defer it.

3) **Clarity**—"What exactly am I offering?"

Vagueness is where "silent ledgers" grow.

Set simple, kind terms upfront: scope, timing, limits.

Example: "I can review two pages tonight and send notes by 8 p.m."

4) **Calibration**—"How much should I give, and to whom?"

Use this rhythm: Open → Clear → Responsive.

- **Open:** Start cooperative.
- **Clear:** Make your cooperation visible. ("I sent the draft—can you proof the slides?")
- **Responsive:** If reciprocity appears, continue. If not, reduce or pause.
- **Reset:** If reciprocity returns later, reset without punishment.

This helps you remain warm without being exposed.

5) **Consequences**—What happens if limits aren't respected?

Have a kind fallback ready. Boundaries protect your ability to keep giving.

- "I can't take this on right now."
- "Happy to help after you complete X."
- "I can do A or B—what would help most?"

If patterns of taking persist, step back without drama.

Practical Toolkit

Red flags to notice (patterns, not one-offs)

- Chronic non-reciprocation
- "Moving goalposts"
- "Guilt-tripping"
- "Last-minute emergencies" becoming the norm
- Boundary-testing after you've been clear

Clean, humane boundary scripts

- "I want to help, and I can offer this part by Friday. For the rest, I'll need you to take the lead."
- "I can be there from 3:00 to 3:30. After that, I'm offline."
- "Let's make this mutual: I'll handle the call if you can send the brief beforehand."

Important nuance

Calibration is not meant to measure who is "worthy."

Use it to pace your giving, not to prove anything. If your inner peace starts hinging on someone else's response, return to the compass: give what aligns, release what depletes.

Mini-exercise: Boundary rehearsal (3 minutes)

- Write one "yes-with-limits" line you can use this week.
- Write one "kind no" you can use this week.
- Say both out loud once today.

Notice how much easier it is to serve when the words are already in your pocket.

When not to calibrate

- **One-off acts (stranger in need):** lead with generosity; there may be no repeat interaction.
- **Power imbalances (caregiving, manager–direct reports):** clarity and boundaries matter more than reciprocity.
- **Harmful dynamics (manipulation, abuse):** step out; your safety is non-negotiable.

Protecting your energy is not unkind—it is what keeps your service sustainable.

A few questions tend to arise at this stage.

Questions

- **Is it selfish to expect acknowledgment for giving?**

Not exactly. Expecting gratitude is human. The problem is not the expectation itself but letting peace depend on it. The "silent ledger" simply shows where the ego is still attached—not failure, but useful feedback.

- **Why does giving sometimes produce resentment rather than joy?**

Because the ego sneaks in with conditions: give, but also receive recognition. When recognition doesn't come, the joy sours—a signal that you've reached the boundary of conditional giving.

- **Should you stop giving when unappreciated?**

No. Stopping shrinks the heart. The path is to notice the expectation, soften it, and practice giving as its own reward. And if others are genuinely taking advantage, boundaries matter. Contributive living is not about permitting exploitation—it is about serving with integrity and choice.

Closing Note and Invitation: The Threshold of Optimization

At the Contributive stage, light shines outward. The quiet joy of giving has been discovered — and so has the subtle pull of expectation. Engagement is strong. Care is wide. Meaning is real.

A 6–5–5 life is active, relational, and purposeful. People at this stage are building, serving, and loving. Work brings prosperity and competence. Relationships bring warmth. Contribution brings significance. Much of what modern life promises is already here.

The person at this stage is not troubled. They have built something real—engagement, relationships, meaning—and they know it. They want to enjoy it fully.

But a quiet question stirs. Not from dissatisfaction. Not from wanting more. From a growing sense that what they have could be better arranged.

"I have built well. But am I living it well? I cannot work harder—that would cost me the very life I am trying to enjoy. And I will not chase more at the expense of what I already have. What I want is to know that my energy is going where it matters most—that nothing important is being quietly neglected, and nothing unimportant is quietly draining me. I want the most from what I have—not more than what I have."

That question is where the next chapter begins.

Chapter 5

The Geometry of Contentment

The Lived Experience: The Case for Contentment

Contentment is not the opposite of ambition. It is the *refinement* of ambition. It is the answer to the question the Contributive person eventually asks: not how do I get more, but how do I get the most from what I already have.

It asks what is worth pursuing now, what is no longer worth the cost, and what trade-offs purchase the most Well-Being per unit of effort.

This is why I call this stage the "Optimized Ego-Based Life." The ego is still present—roles, identity, competence. But instead of endlessly expanding the load, contentment learns to live well inside reality. Not through resignation, but through *intelligent design.*

Contentment does not erase the Well-Being earned through Ambition, Ethics and Contribution. It stabilizes it. It makes it more reliable in ordinary life—especially when circumstances change. You still engage. You still care. But the structure becomes more balanced and therefore more *breathable.*

Practically, this often shows up as a quieter rhythm. You are able to pay attention to the full span of life—work, family, health, friendships, and rejuvenation—without feeling that one area must be sacrificed for another. The beauty of this stage is not in doing less, but in *wasting less.*

A contented life has a distinct feel. It is lighter—not because life has become easy, but because inner effort is no longer wasted in friction. The same responsibilities are carried with more space. The same work is done with less strain. The same care is offered with more warmth.

To understand why this stage becomes so important, we need to look at the most common way Well-Being collapses in adult life: not through irresponsibility, but through sincerity carried beyond its structural capacity. That analysis will take a moment. It may feel like a chapter within a chapter. But without it, Contentment can be misread as a lifestyle preference rather than what it truly is: a *repair of structure.*

When Responsibility Outpaces Inner Space

Many people do not experience a drop in Well-Being because they are careless. They experience it because they are sincere.

They work hard. They stay responsible. They try to live ethically. They care for family. They show up for others. They pay bills, keep promises, and carry more than their share—often without drawing attention to it. From the outside, their life looks like success. From the inside, it feels like *weight.* This part of the chapter is for that person—the one who is doing a lot, and yet feels less alive than they did when they had less.

What makes this stage especially painful is not the work itself, but the contrast. You remember a time when effort brought energy, when caring felt expansive, when responsibility did not feel like a weight. The loss of that *inner aliveness* is rarely spoken about—but it is felt deeply. The fall from a higher Well-Being hurts more than never having tasted it at all. Often, the pain takes the form of simple, private thoughts:

- "I used to be more alive."
- "I used to care without resentment."
- "I used to feel proud of who I was becoming."

These thoughts are not nostalgia. They are *signals.* They appear when there is a particular kind of exhaustion that does not come from laziness or confusion. It comes from *sustained effort without inner space.* You may still be productive, reliable and "good", but something changes quietly.

- Work becomes *duty* rather than *engagement.*
- Family becomes *obligation* rather than *joy.*
- Rest becomes *recovery* rather than *renewal.*
- Success becomes pressure—because it must be maintained.

This is not a personal failure. It is a **structural** one.

- *Activity* is not the same as *Engagement* (Length).
- *Care* is not the same as *Spaciousness* (Width).
- *Responsibility* is not the same as *Stability* (Depth).

When these distinctions blur, Well-Being leaks—even as effort increases.

Story: Ravi's Invisible Burden

Ravi is 42. He is the kind of person people trust. At work, he is dependable. He meets deadlines, solves problems, trains newcomers, and rarely complains. At home, he is steady. He is present for his children, supports his parents, and pays attention to his spouse's needs. He is not drifting. He is not confused about values. He is not irresponsible. And yet, he often feels like he is *dragging himself through his own life.*

He wakes up already tired—not because he slept poorly, but because his mind never fully stops. Even small decisions feel heavy: a repair bill, a school expense, a medical checkup. All day long, Ravi carries a quiet *mental arithmetic:*

- "If I say yes to this, what breaks?"
- "If I say no to that, who gets hurt?"
- "If I take a risk, what do I endanger?"

He knows he has skill. He knows he could likely earn more in a bigger city. He knows part of his fatigue is financial pressure. But each time he considers change, the structure of his life holds him in place. The children are settled. The mortgage is manageable here. His parents depend on him. So he stays. And because he stays, a different struggle begins—not the struggle of survival, but the struggle of meaning. He begins to wonder, quietly and guiltily, whether this is what life will feel like forever: *responsibility without breath.*

Ravi is often praised as a "great guy." Inside, he feels *unseen, tired,* and occasionally *resentful*—then ashamed of that resentment.

People like Ravi rarely ask for help. Their identity is built on being the one who manages.

How Well-Being Declines Here

Ravi did not arrive here through a single mistake. His situation unfolded gradually, through ordinary, well-intentioned steps.

1. The "Expansion Trap": Ravi spent his 30s building a "Good Life." He advanced his career, bought a larger home for the growing family, and ensured his kids had every opportunity. This was the right thing to do. But with every upgrade came a new baseline. The mortgage, the tuitions, the parent care, the neighborhood status—the container grew larger, and it demanded to be filled. Suddenly, the *Optional* became *Essential.*

2. The Loss of the "Joy of Contribution": There was a time when helping others fueled him. But as expenses mounted and time vanished, Contribution stopped being a source of energy and became a tax on his time. He still contributes—he is a responsible man—but he does it with a heavy heart. He helps his team, but secretly resents the time it takes away from his own work. He cares for his parents, but feels the weight of the duty. The act remains, but the *nourishment* is gone. The added depth that came from the joy of contribution is no longer there.

3. The "Hot Burn" of Engagement: Now, the pressure is on. The expenses must be met. Ravi shifts into a "Win at All Costs" mentality. He needs the bonus. He needs the promotion. His Engagement increases (he is working furiously), but the motivation has shifted from *Purpose* to *Panic.* He becomes transactional. He is too stressed to be generous, too anxious to be principled, and too pressured to practice moderation. His inner stability that came from integrity, non-injury and moderation is now entirely *mortgaged* to external outcomes. If the bonus comes, he breathes. If it doesn't, he breaks.

This is the condition of the modern "Sincere Struggler."

- **High Effort:** Much doing, without *aliveness.*
- **High Responsibility:** Much caring, with strain.
- **Low Well-Being:** Not enough depth to carry the load.

It is not a failure of character. It is a failure of physics. He is trying to carry a massive load with an inner structure that has quietly thinned. It is from this point—not from laziness, but from honest exhaustion—that a deeper question begins to surface: Is there a way to carry responsibility without carrying it so heavily?

How Contentment Takes Shape

Contentment grows when effort, expectations, and means are brought into honest alignment. It is not a change in values, but a reorganization of how those values are carried in daily life.

What follows is not a prescription, but a pattern that appears whenever Contentment stabilizes.

1. Restoring Dignity Before Change

Before any practical adjustment can work, *dignity* must be restored.

Many responsible people carry an unspoken belief: "If I were doing better, I wouldn't feel this tired." That belief quietly erodes self-respect. It turns every conversation into a defense and every suggestion into a threat.

The stabilizing realization is simple and grounding: "I am not failing. I am carrying my share."

With dignity restored, conversations soften. Choices become possible again—not because constraints vanish, but because self-blame no longer dominates the inner landscape.

2. Making Constraints Explicit

Contentment does not begin with change. It begins with *visibility.*

Many constraints feel immovable simply because they are carried silently:

- "My spouse does not want to work."
- "A large home is necessary."
- "Relocation is not an option."

When such constraints remain unspoken, they press inward. When they are *named*—calmly and without accusation—they move from the mind into the shared space of dialogue.

Contentment begins here: not by removing limits, but by seeing them clearly.

3. Testing Assumptions Gently

Once constraints are visible, assumptions can be tested—without urgency or rebellion.

- "If we downsize, will the children truly suffer?"
  (Often, children value calm parents more than square footage.)
- "If we reduce expenses, what freedom do we buy back?"

This stage is exploratory, not corrective. The goal is not to prove that change is required, but to discover what actually matters. Many families find that emotional continuity and presence matter far more than the scale of their surroundings.

4. Accepting What Remains (Without Resentment)

Some constraints will not move.

A spouse may not want to relocate. Aging parents may require proximity. Health may limit energy or options. Contentment does not demand that these realities disappear. It asks only that they be accepted *after* exploration—not *before.*

This distinction matters. Acceptance that follows *inquiry* stabilizes Depth. Acceptance that precedes inquiry breeds resentment.

When acceptance is conscious, energy stops leaking into "if only" fantasies and returns to the present. This is where inner stability quietly strengthens.

5. Balancing Within Reality

With dignity restored, constraints clarified, assumptions tested, and acceptance grounded, something opens: choice within limits.

This is where Contentment becomes active rather than passive.

- Expenses are simplified—not to punish life, but to buy time.
- Work is approached with renewed craft—not to climb, but to enjoy mastery.
- Leisure becomes local and relational—not performative.

Externally, little may change. Internally, life becomes breathable again. Effort and reward begin to feel proportional. Roles are inhabited rather than endured.

6. Reclaiming Rhythm

What emerges is not a smaller life, but a *right-sized* one.

Daily life regains rhythm. Peace is no longer postponed to a future condition. This is the geometry of Contentment: not escape, not settling, but *alignment.*

The story that follows illustrates this pattern with a cooperative partner. Not everyone has that. For those navigating these adjustments alone—without a partner to share the load, or with constraints that cannot be redistributed—the same six steps apply, but steps two and three carry more weight. Making constraints visible and testing assumptions may require a trusted friend, a counselor, or simply honest journaling rather than dialogue. The destination is the same: clarity that restores dignity and makes choice possible again.

Story: Contentment Under Load

Amy is 41. She is a homemaker in a modest coastal town. Her days are full: cooking, cleaning, managing schedules, driving children to activities, volunteering at the local church, helping at the food bank. She has never been idle. Her life is not glamorous—but it is intentional.

For years, it felt light.

Then John's parents needed to move in.

They were aging. One needed daily assistance. Medical appointments increased. Medication schedules became complex. The house felt smaller—not physically, but emotionally.

Amy adjusted, as she always had.

She absorbed the added tasks. She reorganized the kitchen. She managed the appointments. She reduced her volunteering. She slept less.

At first, she told herself this was temporary.

But slowly, something changed.

The joy that once accompanied her giving began to thin. She still cared. She still acted. But she felt stretched. Her in-laws, preoccupied with their own discomfort, rarely expressed gratitude. The work became invisible.

She noticed something subtle: she was no longer tired from effort. She was tired from *carrying effort alone.*

That honest observation was the beginning.

Amy did not accuse. She did not collapse. She did something quieter.

She acknowledged two truths at once:

- "I am doing my best."
- "And this structure is no longer sustainable."

That clarity allowed a different kind of conversation.

One evening, she sat with John—not in resentment, but in alignment.

She did not ask him to "fix" his parents. She did not dramatize her exhaustion. She described the load. She named the erosion of joy. She said she wanted to continue caring—but not at the cost of becoming *brittle.*

They adjusted.

John began spending an hour each evening with his parents, fully present. Not multitasking. Not distracted.

Amy reclaimed that hour for herself—sometimes a walk, sometimes quiet reading, sometimes simply sitting in silence.

They arranged for a caregiver to come four hours each week. Not only to ease the practical load—but to protect something equally important: their marriage.

Those few hours became *sacred.* Sometimes they walked along the shoreline. Sometimes they sat in a quiet café. Sometimes they said very little at all. But they were together—not as caregivers, not as parents, not as problem-solvers—just as Amy and John.

That space revitalized them.

Amy's regained steadiness softened the atmosphere of the home. Her in-laws noticed the difference. The sharpness that had crept in during moments of fatigue faded. Conversations grew warmer. Small expressions of appreciation began to surface—not dramatic declarations, but simple acknowledgments: "We know this isn't easy. Thank you."

Gratitude, once absent, began to circulate.

The work had not disappeared. The responsibilities remained. But the rhythm changed.

Instead of strain feeding silence, *steadiness fed appreciation.* Appreciation fed connection. Connection fed energy.

A new equilibrium formed—not lighter in responsibility, but lighter in experience.

This is how Contentment stabilizes itself.

It does not remove life's weight. It *redistributes* it—until *care feels like choice* again.

Contentment is not the reduction of responsibility. It is the intelligent arrangement of it.

It restores presence without restlessness, care without strain, and enoughness without defensiveness.

Nothing about her life is dramatic. And that is precisely the point.

Ravi and Amy represent the harder cases—where strain has already appeared and structure needs repair. But Contentment serves a third person too: the one whose life is broadly working, who has built well, and who simply wants the formation to run better. For that person the same six steps apply—not as repair but as tuning. And the result, when it comes, has a distinct quality. Not dramatic. Not euphoric. But deeply satisfying—the quiet pleasure of a life running in formation, all its elements finally pulling together, in a rhythm that holds and a fullness that does not need to prove itself.

The Geometry

Length—Extent of Engagement (Score: 6)

Amy is fully engaged. Her days are active and responsibility is real. She cooks, coordinates, supports aging parents, guides her children, and maintains the home. But her engagement is rhythmic *rather* than *reactive.*

She no longer confuses constant output with devotion. She protects space for recovery. She adjusts structures when strain appears. Effort flows in cycles—exertion and renewal—instead of running in one continuous surge.

Her energy is not reduced. It is *regulated.*

This is where effort-based engagement reaches its fullest, most sustainable expression. The score is the same as in Ambition—but the quality is entirely different. In Ambition, six represented the maximum the engine could produce before overheating. Here, six is the natural rhythm of a life in genuine proportion: fully engaged within the real limits of human energy, without cost to recovery or relationship.

Width—Scope of Identification (Score: 6)

Amy's circle of care is wide—family, in-laws, children, community—but it is no longer carried alone. She invites participation. She communicates honestly. Care becomes collaborative rather than sacrificial.

Her warmth is practical, embodied, and sincere. She does not attempt to save everyone, nor does she close her heart to those who need her. By redistributing responsibility, her care remains generous without becoming brittle.

Her relationships are not drains; they are exchanges.

Width at this stage is real and generous. The contented person has built their circle with care: family, community, causes, perhaps a faith or a nation. They love it well and tend it faithfully.

Depth—Source of Stability (Score: 6)

Contentment adds one further source of Depth: the calm that comes from acting in genuine proportion to one's capacity—not heroically, not self-suppressingly, but in rhythm with what life actually asks and what the self can sustainably offer. This is not the same as non-harm or moderation, which reduced friction and cost. *Calibrated calm* is what remains when friction is low and cost is managed: a quiet sufficiency that does not need to prove itself or defend itself. This is the deepest stability the *self-managed* life can reach. It holds under ordinary pressure.

Volume of Well-Being: 6 × 6 × 6 = 216

Why Life Feels More Alive When It Is Balanced

A balanced life does more than stabilize numbers—it changes the texture of daily experience. When engagement is held at its maximum, there is little room left. Life becomes dense. Every moment is allocated. Even meaningful activities feel tight. When engagement is moderated and supported by equal care and stability, space returns. There is room to breathe.

- Room for a relaxed morning walk.
- Room to sit quietly with a partner and watch a show without thinking of the next task.
- Room to notice the sky, the light, the flowers—things that were always present, but rarely registered.

Nothing essential has been lost. Productivity remains. Purpose remains. Contribution remains. What disappears is the constant internal compression. This is why Contentment feels like enoughness. Not because life has shrunk, but because life is no longer overcrowded. A life that breathes is a life that can grow.

This sense of enoughness is not the end of development. It is the foundation for the next stages—where expansion no longer risks collapse, because the structure beneath it is stable.

The Structural Limit of Contentment

Contentment represents the highest optimization of an ego-centered life.

At this stage, life is well-managed. Desires are calibrated. Resources are aligned. Boundaries are clear. Effort, care, and stability support one another in dynamic equilibrium. Like a well-tuned engine, the system runs smoothly.

Yet the very balance that produced this rise in Well-Being now begins to define its ceiling.

Contentment stabilizes life. It does not expand it indefinitely.

The Limit of Engagement (Score 6):

Engagement remains steady and rhythmic. Life is active, meaningful, and proportionate.

But engagement still follows preference.

The ego engages deeply where it finds interest, meaning, or identity. There will always be moments—caregiving when exhausted, duties without inspiration—where action is sustained by responsibility rather than flow.

As long as life is organized around the self, engagement cannot become *universal* or *frictionless.*

It can be *harmonious*—but not *boundless.*

The Limit of Width (Score 6):

Width, too, reaches a natural plateau.

Care has expanded beyond the self to include partner, children, friends, and community. The heart is open and generous—but still selective.

Love flows toward what resonates. Toward what aligns with identity and values. Toward "my circle."

To widen further would require identification that is no longer organized around personal belonging.

Contentment softens the ego. It does not *dissolve* it.

The Limit of Depth (Score 6): Depth at this stage is strong. You are resilient to ordinary pressures. Integrity has reduced internal friction. Non-injury has softened reactivity. Moderation has restored rhythm. Contribution has added meaning. Contentment has brought peace.

But this stability remains *self-referenced.*

Peace is sustained through ongoing calibration—of health, finances, relationships, time, and energy. As long as equilibrium depends on successful management by the self, it remains *conditionally stable.*

A sudden shock—severe illness, profound loss, systemic collapse—can still overwhelm the structure. Not because the person is weak, but because the *center of gravity* remains tied to the continuity of the self's arrangements.

That is why it stabilizes at 6.

To go further, stability must no longer depend on the preservation of the self's design.

The Geometry of Potential

The result is a stable, peaceful, and genuinely happy life—often with a Well-Being volume around 216.

Compared to the turbulence of Ambition or the strain of imbalance, this is a profound achievement.

And yet, the geometry quietly reveals something startling.

The theoretical potential of Well-Being is 1000 (10 × 10 × 10).

Even at its best, the ego-centered life reaches only a fraction of what is structurally possible.

Contentment does not conceal this gap.

It *reveals* it.

Closing Note and Invitation: Contentment as a Foundation

One quiet effect of Contentment is worth naming before moving forward. As inner strain reduces, the anxiety around scarcity loosens. From this ground of sufficiency, giving becomes easier and more natural—not from obligation but from *enoughness.* And that giving, in turn, deepens Contentment itself. It returns as purpose, gratitude, and connection. This is not a strategy. It is a structural effect: reduced resistance allows care to flow outward, and that outward flow stabilizes the very contentment from which it arose.

Contentment is not where growth ends. It is where ego-based growth completes.

Here, effort becomes sustainable. Care becomes nourishing. Stability becomes reliable. Life breathes.

If you find yourself here, understand this clearly: You have optimized everything the self can optimize.

What remains cannot be accessed through better management, sharper trade-offs, or finer calibration of desire.

To move beyond this point, new sources of Depth, Width, and Engagement must be discovered—not by expanding the self, but by *seeing through it.*

This is not a call to dissatisfaction.

It is an invitation to *curiosity.*

Balance does not close doors. It opens them.

A life that has learned how to carry itself well is finally ready to explore what lies beyond the self.

That exploration is the subject of the chapters ahead.

Interlude

The Physics of Resistance

The Next Constraint

The stages behind us have accomplished something real. Inertia gave way to Ambition. Ambition was refined by Ethics. Ethics overflowed into Contribution. And Contribution was harmonized by Contentment. The structure is now balanced, proportionate, and *breathable.* This is no small achievement.

And yet, something remains. Even in a well-balanced life, effort still carries *tension.* Action still carries *anxiety.* Failure still stings. Success still fades. The *background hum* of "I hope this works" has quieted—but it has not disappeared.

So a deeper question naturally arises: Is this the best Well-Being a responsible, engaged life can offer? Or is there a way for Well-Being itself to deepen—without increasing effort?

Because effort is no longer the variable we can turn up.

When Effort Is No Longer the Lever

Occasionally, we encounter people who seem to live by a different internal physics.

- They act fully, yet without *strain.*
- They respond to failure without bitterness.
- They recover from disturbance almost instantly.

They are not withdrawn. They are not passive. And they are not exerting more effort than we are. So what is different? At this stage, the question is no longer: "How can I do better?" It becomes: "What is resisting life inside me?"

To understand this shift, we need a different lens.

The Missing Variable: A Physics of Well-Being

In physics, **Ohm's Law** describes the relationship between three forces:

1. **Voltage (*V*):** The *driving potential.*
2. **Current (*I*):** The *flow that results.*
3. **Resistance (*R*):** The *opposition within the system.*

The law is simple:

$$I = \frac{V}{R}$$

The Insight: For a given voltage, current does not increase by pushing harder. It increases when resistance drops.

Human Well-Being follows a similar structure. We can map it this way:

$$W = \frac{E}{R}$$

- ***W* (Well-Being):** The lived quality of your experience (The Flow).
- ***E* (Energy):** The total life force you bring to the moment.
- ***R* (Resistance):** The internal opposition you carry (Ego, Friction, Clinging).

Up to now, we have focused on the Numerator (*E*). We have increased Engagement (Length). We have widened Identification (Width). We have strengthened Stability (Depth). The geometry has expanded and balanced.

At the stage of Contentment, the structure is strong. It is proportionate. It holds.

But it still has *edges.*

Imagine the geometry of Contentment as a large *cuboid*—balanced along all three axes. It is stable. It stands firmly. But its faces press against the world. It has corners. It has friction.

That friction is subtle. It is not chaos. It is attachment. It is the carefully assembled life we now call "mine." My work. My relationships. My values. My way of being.

Nothing here is wrong. It is mature. It is earned.

But the structure still resists movement.

To move further, we do not expand the cuboid. We *smooth* it.

As friction reduces, the edges soften. The corners round. The rigid faces give way to a continuous surface.

The shape becomes *spherical.*

A sphere is not unstable. In fact, it is one of the most structurally stable forms in nature. It distributes force evenly. It has no weak corners. It *rolls without preference.*

Its minimal points of contact reduce resistance.

This is the next refinement of Well-Being. Not greater effort. Not greater expansion. But reduced friction.

Life continues to expand. But attachment to particular outcomes and identities softens.

This is what reducing Resistance (R) truly means.

Why This Changes Everything

In $W = E / R$, when Resistance (R) is high, even great Effort (E) produces only modest Well-Being (W). But as Resistance softens, the same Effort yields disproportionately more Peace. Resistance has no *floor*—as it approaches zero, Well-Being increases beyond what Effort alone could ever produce.

- Every moment of *defensiveness, possessiveness,* or *self-protection* adds Resistance.
- Every moment of *openness, acceptance,* and *non-clinging* reduces Resistance.

This is not philosophy. It is an experiment you can run immediately.

What a Low-Resistance Life Feels Like

When inner resistance drops, the change is not dramatic. It is structural. It shows up in the texture of daily experience as increased inner stability and greater ease in responding to life.

You begin to notice:

- **Inner Stability**
  - Irritation dissolves quickly.
  - Success does not inflate you; failure does not fracture you.
  - Joy and sorrow still occur—but they pass through without *residue.*
  - You rest easily—because nothing inside is being *gripped.*
  - A quiet contentment remains, even when circumstances fluctuate.
- **Outward Availability**
  - You act fully—and now without inner tightening.
  - You do not feel compelled to defend your identity in every disagreement.

- You are naturally friendly and approachable, because you are not guarding *territory.*
- Compassion arises naturally—not as *performance,* but as *reflex.*
- You find yourself available to more of life's contexts—not only the ones that favor you.

Nothing dramatic has been added. Friction has simply been reduced.

The next stages of this book are not about doing more. They are about removing the friction that blocks the flow.

What Comes Next

The chapters that follow explore three frameworks for reducing resistance. They have roots in ancient inquiry, but what this book draws on is their structural logic—not their metaphysical claims. Each has been observed independently across cultures precisely because each addresses something real in human experience. No prior knowledge or belief is required—only the willingness to observe your own inner state honestly.

They work on three distinct layers:

1. **Non-Attachment:** Reducing resistance in Action—the *friction of attachment to results.*
2. **Contemplation:** Reducing the *friction of a scattered mind.*
3. **Self-Inquiry:** Reducing resistance in Identity—the *friction of a fixed self.*

Each works on a different layer of resistance. Together, they point to a possibility that effort alone could never reach.

Chapter 6

The Geometry of Non-Attachment

Action Without Resistance

In the interlude before this chapter, we encountered a crucial insight: *effort* has practical limits.

You can refine ambition, act ethically, contribute generously, and even optimize your life through contentment—yet still notice tension in action, anxiety around outcomes, and subtle agitation that never fully disappears.

If Well-Being is to deepen further, the lever is no longer the numerator (more effort). It is the denominator: less inner *resistance*.

The first disciplined method for reducing that resistance is action without *attachment*—remaining fully active in life while releasing the emotional grip on results. This is what this chapter explores in structural terms.

The Hidden Source of Resistance

So far, we have tried to improve our inner state largely through doing: achieving, behaving ethically, helping others, fulfilling responsibilities. All of this helps—but none of it fully quiets the mind. Why?

Because the very impulse to act is often entangled with resistance.

You may recognize the signs:

- feverishness before beginning,
- restlessness while waiting,
- emotional swings after outcomes arrive.

Even when results are favorable, satisfaction fades quickly, and a new urge takes its place. This is where the inward investigation begins—not into actions themselves, but into the *machinery* of action and reaction. What we discover is a powerful engine behind resistance: the accumulated weight of past reactions. Every action, desire, and emotional reaction leaves an impression—a trace in the subconscious that accumulates into habitual tendencies. Like *grooves* worn into a path, these tendencies pull the mind in familiar directions without conscious choice. In the tradition this chapter draws on, these impressions are called **Vasanas**—a precise term for something most of us have experienced but rarely named.

Here is the key connection to our new lens:

Vasanas are not just memories. They are the inner forces that generate resistance.

They are what make the mind cling, fear, chase, replay, and avoid.

The mechanism is simple and observable:

1. Pleasant experiences leave positively charged impressions → later returning as *desire.*
2. Painful experiences leave negatively charged impressions → later returning as *aversion.*
3. Neutral experiences leave little trace → they do not resurface.

This is why much of daily life passes unnoticed, while certain moments replay again and again. Each time action is driven by attachment—through craving, fear, pride, or self-image—the groove deepens:

- positive outcomes keep us *chasing,*
- negative outcomes keep us *avoiding.*

The mind remains pulled and pushed. Resistance regenerates. As long as this continues, Well-Being struggles to deepen—not because life is wrong, but because resistance keeps rebuilding itself from within, from the Vasanas.

Reducing Resistance at the Source

This practice of non-attachment offers a practical science for weakening this machinery at its source.

When action is performed with attachment—to desire, outcome, or identity—the impression left behind carries a strong emotional charge. That charge strengthens future urges. Resistance grows.

When action is performed without attachment—neither clinging to the act nor to its result—the impression left behind is closer to neutral. Neutral impressions have less force. Old grooves begin to soften.

Put simply:

- Attachment → *scored impression* → stronger push/pull → higher resistance
- *Offering* → *neutral impression* → less reactivity → lower resistance

This is why this practice emphasizes responsibility and service. It is easier to act with neutrality when action arises from what life asks—family, work, community—rather than from self-centered craving.

Non-attachment is not resignation. It is *intelligent living:* act fully, serve well, and let action itself become the means of reducing resistance.

One might assume that simply doing less—non-action—would achieve the same result. It does not. Non-action does not dissolve resistance. Even when the body is still, the mind remains active—shaped by Vasanas that continue to agitate and pull. Avoidance often strengthens resistance, intensifying inner restlessness rather than quieting it. Instead of promoting inner stability and outward availability, it can quietly erode both.

Non-Attachment Does Not Reduce Excellence

A natural fear arises at this point: "If I act without attachment to outcomes, will I lose passion, productivity, or excellence?"

In practice, the opposite is often true. Attachment can generate energy—but it also generates inner noise: fear, clinging, self-protection, and identity-stakes. That noise clouds judgment.

A surgeon is not allowed to operate on a spouse—not because care is lacking, but because emotional attachment impairs clarity. A judge recuses themselves from a case involving family for the same reason.

It is not care that interferes—it is attachment.

Non-attachment is full engagement without inner *clutching.*

A nurse caring for a child is attentive and compassionate, yet not *possessive.* When the parent arrives, the nurse hands the child over easily. The quality of care remains clean and steady.

This is a central insight of this stage:

Non-attachment does not reduce excellence. It removes the inner resistance that *sabotages* it.

Passion fueled by attachment *burns hot and burns out.* Engagement grounded in non-attachment *burns steady*—supporting focus, resilience, and clarity.

Non-Attachment vs. Resilience

In modern self-help, resilience is often treated as the peak virtue: endure setbacks, recover, keep striving. It's noble—and necessary. But resilience alone does not guarantee inner peace. Resilience is powered by determination to reach a goal. It keeps the mind tied to outcomes: success soothes, failure disturbs.

The practice of non-attachment refines that same strength. You still strive with full effort, but peace does not depend on results. Each attempt becomes inner training—reducing ego, softening resistance.

A clean contrast:

- The resilient person is a master of *endurance.*
- The practitioner of non-attachment is a master of *equanimity.*

Resilience can keep you moving on the *treadmill* of desire. Non-attachment gradually dismantles the treadmill itself. Resilience works on outcomes. Non-attachment works on Vasanas—the inner circuitry that keeps outcomes emotionally charged.

Duty Reimagined: From Burden to Service

Traditionally, this practice of non-attachment is taught as duty: do your duty without attachment. While powerful, this framing can still feel heavy. The ego finds new footholds:

- "Why am *I* always doing this?"
- "Why don't *others* do their share?"

Here is the clarifying shift:

Duty often generates resistance ("Why me?"). Service dissolves resistance ("This is my practice.").

The outer action may be identical, but the inner experience changes completely when duty is reframed as service.

The Chef's Kitchen: A Living Philosophy of Action

Imagine life as a restaurant kitchen.

- You are the chef—skilled, attentive, fully present.
- You are not the owner—you do not carry the weight of profits, reviews, or reputation.

- The restaurant is your life—its hours are your roles and responsibilities.
- The customers are the world—placing orders through family, work, and circumstance.
- The *recipe* is your practice—cook with care, then release the dish.

You do not hover for applause. You do not cling to praise. You cook, serve, and let go. And every sustainable kitchen shares one discipline: it *closes.* That is not laziness. It is rhythm.

Recharging the Instrument

Non-attachment is often mistaken for endless giving. But service without renewal loses its sanctity. In earlier stages, desire supplied fuel. In this practice, the two common motivators—*craving* and *reward*—are removed. Without replenishment, fatigue invites resentment, scorekeeping, and renewed resistance.

Recharging is not optional. It is part of the discipline. Recharge may take many forms—solitude, nature, music, silence, time with loved ones. The test is simple:

Does this reduce dependence on stimulation—or increase it?

True recharge restores inner fullness. It leaves you calm, clear, and available to serve again.

Over time, as Vasanas soften, joy begins to arise from within. Service feels less like *expenditure* and more like *flow.*

What if There Are No Orders?

Sometimes life feels quiet. No obvious asks. No urgent need. In the early stages of this practice, engagement still matters because service reveals ego. Without engagement, certain resistances remain *dormant:* grudges, preferences, impatience, scorekeeping. Service brings them to the surface where they can be softened.

When the chef has no orders, they clean counters, sharpen knives, prep ingredients. In the same way, when life presents no immediate "orders," stay available through small service-oriented tasks—not frantically, but willingly.

The Scale of Service: Large Impact or Daily Humility?

People often wonder about scale. Is "real" service measured by impact?

Large-scale service can uplift many and deserves admiration. But the practice of non-attachment measures something subtler: *purity of attitude.*

Sometimes home is the most rigorous training ground—chores, caregiving, patience—because ego resists the mundane.

And scale carries a quiet risk:

Scale can inflate ego—and *ego is resistance.*

Sometimes public service becomes a refuge from the humility of private service.

So which is better—big or small?

Neither.

The real question is:

Where is the ego dissolving? Where is resistance reducing?

Expanding the Field of Play Through Non-Attachment

Non-attachment frees you to engage in any action, any place, any role—without inner feverishness.

Release attachment to *outcomes* and anxiety *drops.* Your energy is less split. Focus improves. Creativity increases. Passion becomes steadier.

Release attachment to *roles* and your field of play *expands.* You become more available to what the moment calls for.

Detachment is not passivity. It is *availability without inner resistance.*

Misconceptions About Non-Attachment

1) "Non-attachment means you shouldn't have goals." Action needs direction. A teacher aims for students to learn. A doctor aims for healing. The difference is that the practitioner of non-attachment treats these as borrowed goals—taken from life's needs, not ego's cravings.

2) "Non-attachment makes you cold." Detachment is not indifference; it is freedom from possessiveness. It allows deeper compassion because love is no longer tangled with control and fear.

3) "If results don't matter, effort doesn't matter." In the practice of non-attachment, excellence is part of the practice. You offer your best not to prove yourself, but to serve.

The Unshakable Foundation: Equanimity

The ultimate fruit of non-attachment is equanimity: steadiness amid life's dualities—praise and blame, success and failure, pleasure and pain.

The person at this stage is not numb. They still feel. But the waves no longer toss them. They rise, pass, and the center holds. From this steadiness, the deeper qualities of the journey begin to take root.

The Geometry

Length—Extent of Engagement (Score: 8)

In Contentment, engagement stayed at six. Action wasn't the problem—friction was. As resistance drops, we are open to more of life. We are now responding rather than increasing effort. The engine can now run fast, but stay cool.

This is where the nature of Length itself changes. Up to this point, Length measured *directed effort*—the proportion of waking energy consciously organized toward purposeful action. That form of engagement has been optimized. It cannot grow further by adding hours or increasing intensity. What grows from here is something different: the range of life the person can meet with full presence. As the *preference-filter* loosens—as the distinction between roles I choose and roles life assigns begins to dissolve—the field of *available engagement* widens without requiring more effort. Length no longer measures how hard the person works. It measures how openly they are available to what the moment asks.

Width—Scope of Identification (Score: 8)

In Contentment, our care often stays within "what I like" or "what is mine." Non-attachment loosens that filter. If life sends an order (a difficult colleague, a mundane chore), they meet it with the same steadiness as a passion project. As "I like / I dislike" loses its authority, the heart widens to include much more of reality.

Width at this stage expands in two distinct movements, which is why the gain is larger here than at surrounding stages. The first movement is from my world to the *relatable world:* as preference loses its grip, empathy begins to extend beyond what was chosen or owned—to people and causes that are not "mine", but that I can still recognize and feel for. The second movement goes further: compassion begins to arise from a position of *neutrality* rather than *affinity.* The person at this stage is compassionate by default, and remains so until—and this is the honest limit of this stage—something genuinely challenges their values or beliefs. At that point, the heart may still close. The filter has not disappeared; it has simply receded. These two movements together account for the full width gain at this stage. What remains is the work of making that neutrality unconditional—which belongs to the chapter that follows.

Depth—Source of Stability (Score: 8)

Non-attachment deepens Depth through two qualitatively new shifts—which is why the gain here, like at Ethics, is larger than at surrounding stages. The first is *independence from results:* not better tolerance of bad outcomes, but a genuine change in the relationship to outcomes altogether. The inner state is no longer *hostage* to whether the action succeeds. Stability is now sourced in the quality of engagement itself, and the world does not need to *cooperate* for peace to remain intact. The second is *independence from the specific field of action:* the person at this stage is no longer confined to a particular role or domain in order to find meaning and steadiness. The teacher who can wash the floor with the same quality of attention as teaching a class has freed themselves from a subtle but real constraint—the identity that said "I am only fully myself in this role." Together, these two shifts open a field of stability that is no longer defined by what happens, or by who is doing it.

The Volume of Well-Being: 8 × 8 × 8 = 512

The score rises not because life demands more hours, but because more of life can now be met without resistance. This is not a constant lived state; it is the stability this stage makes possible when practice is consistent. The essential insight is simple: by reducing the friction of "me," Well-Being can rise dramatically—without turning up effort.

Concrete Tools for Stabilizing Non-Attachment

1. **The Diagnostic Tool: FIR**[1]

   How do you measure progress in reducing friction? Use FIR to track reactive states (anger, anxiety, disappointment):

   - **Frequency:** How often does it arise? (Daily → Weekly?)
   - **Intensity:** How strong is the grip? (Rage → Irritation?)
   - **Recoverability:** How quickly do you return to center? (Days → Minutes?)

   This isn't about suppressing emotion. It's about reducing its structural drag—so the grip shortens and the mind recovers faster.

2. **The Daily Practice: The Three-Act Play**

   Treat any significant task (a meeting, a chore, a conversation) as a three-part ritual:

   - **Act 1 (Intention):** "I offer this action to serve."

[1] I first encountered the FIR framework through a friend who had heard it attributed to Swami Paramarthananda.

- **Act 2 (Action):** Perform with full focus and excellence.
- **Act 3 (Release):** "I have done my part; the results are not mine."

3. **The Micro-Practice: The Small Act**

The ego often prefers "big impact" because it feeds identity. To dissolve ego, practice the small:

- Choose one invisible task (washing a dish, picking up trash).
- Do it with the care of a surgeon.
- Notice the mind saying, "This is beneath me."
- Do it anyway—and watch what softens.

The Structural Limit

The practice of non-attachment is a massive leap. It liberates action. But it has a limit. The limit is *extroversion.*

Non-attachment quiets the mind through action. It needs an "order" to cook.

- The practitioner is peaceful while serving.
- But when the kitchen closes completely—when there is no action, no role, no duty—the mind may still not know how to be silent.

We have removed resistance from the *hand.* But it may still linger in the *gaze.* To go further, we must learn to quiet the mind directly.

Closing Note and Invitation

Non-attachment does not ask you to renounce life. It asks you to *renounce the friction.*

Every task becomes practice. Every relationship becomes training. You act with excellence—and release ownership.

With resistance reduced in action, you are now ready to turn inward—to explore the subtler layers of attention and identity themselves. This is where the next chapter begins.

Chapter 7

The Geometry of Contemplation

The Next Hiding Place of Resistance

In the previous chapter, we made a decisive move. We realized that increasing the numerator (Effort) had hit a ceiling, so we turned toward the denominator (Resistance). Through the practice of non-attachment, we reduced a major source of resistance: the friction that comes from outcomes. By letting go of the fruit of action, we greatly reduced the drag of anxiety, disappointment, and fear of failure. You might think the work is done. You are active, ethical, and unbothered by results. But if you look closely, there is still a hum of agitation.

Why?

The Tyranny of the Impulse: You have dealt with the result of action, but you have not dealt with the source of action. Even the practitioner of non-attachment is constantly driven to act. The mind is perpetually generating orders:

- "This needs fixing."
- "That person needs help."
- "This situation is incorrect."

Who is deciding these things? Your Mind. Up until now, you have been a loyal servant to your mind. When it said "Achieve," you achieved. When it said "Serve," you served. You have optimized your life, but you have done it under the constant commentary of your own thoughts.

This reveals the next layer of resistance: The resistance to *stillness.* As long as you are compelled to act—driven by your mind's judgments of what is "right," "worthy," or "necessary"—you are not free. You are merely a skilled responder. You are reacting to the world, not resting in it. If we want to move closer to the potential of 1000, we have to make this remaining friction visible. We need to break the link between the *Impulse* and the *Reaction.* We need to learn to sit with the mind, watch its frantic commands, and, for the first time, choose not to follow.

The Inner Lake: The Shift from Outside-In to Inside-Out

But how does this look in lived experience? Meditation is the first time we directly experience this shift. When we learn to observe the mind—to quiet it, steady it, and hold it under gentle control—we discover something evident: we are alive as an awareness beyond the mind. This isn't theory. It is lived experience. It is about peace, and a Well-Being that needs nothing outside.

Life until now has felt *outside-in*: a chasing of joy in objects, achievements, or recognition. But in meditation, we find that the model is *inside-out.* Within us lies a lake of joy—at its depth, something clear and steady. When the waters are still, that clarity shines, and joy arises on its own.

Most of us, longing for glimpses of joy, throw *clay* into the muddied water—a new possession, a bigger achievement, a louder distraction. For a moment, the surface clears, the crystal flashes—and then the water grows even *murkier* than before. Next time, more clay is needed for less joy. This is the treadmill of desire.

Meditation offers another path: do not add more clay, clear the lake. By reducing the accumulated weight of habitual reactions and stilling the turbulence at its depths, the water clears. When it is calm, the crystal shines steadily. Joy is revealed not as something earned but as something *uncovered*—present already, though often unnoticed.

This is why even a few minutes of genuine stillness can feel different from hours of restless effort. And it is why, over time, deeper and longer meditation reshapes life at its roots.

Mind Masquerading as Will

If the "Lake of Joy" is already there, why is it so hard to stop throwing clay into it? Because we are under an illusion. We believe we are already masters of our minds.

In the ambitious stages, your mind felt like a powerful tool—the engine of achievement. You relied on *Willpower.* But in the quiet of meditation, you come to a humbling realization: What you called Willpower was often just the mind changing *disguises.*

When you resist one desire, the mind often slips in another. You resist the urge to complain, only to indulge in the urge to judge. You stop scrolling your phone only to immediately check your email. The mind does not care what it does—noble or trivial—as long as it keeps moving. It fears stillness more than it fears failure.

The 30-Second Test: Do not take my word for it. Test your authority right now. Sit quietly. Close your eyes. Decide to have no thoughts for just thirty seconds.

Almost immediately, the rebellion begins.

- It invents an itch.
- It remembers an email.
- It proposes a "better way" to meditate.

It pretends to be helpful ("Let's make good use of this time"), but its true intent is survival. In that moment, the mask falls. You see that you are not the master; you are a weary soldier in a war that cannot be won by force.

True Will: This is where the definition of strength changes. True will is not the force to do. It is the strength to *see.*

Freedom is not the license to follow every impulse of the mind. Freedom is the power to *hear* the command, feel the *pull,* and *remain perfectly still.*

The Wild Horse: Understanding the Untamed Mind

You now realize that your mind is like a *wild, untamed horse.* For most of your life, it has dragged you wherever it pleased. It never tires—constantly producing thoughts, worries, memories, and scenarios. It replays conversations from years ago, imagines futures that may never happen, and invents problems where none exist.

We are so used to this constant chatter that we mistake it for ourselves. We identify with it: "I am my thoughts." This misidentification—this ignorance of our deeper nature—is the root of suffering. When the horse is restless, we feel restless. When it is fearful, we feel fearful.

The mind does this because it has been trained to stay busy. It constantly seeks stimulation, a problem to solve, a thought to latch onto. Even when you decide to be still, the mind throws up reminders and worries—like a restless horse circling its paddock.

This is not failure. This is the mind doing what it has practiced for a lifetime. But contemplation teaches a new relationship with this horse. You are not the horse; you are the *awareness that observes it.* The practice is not to stop the mind from running or to force it into silence, but to step back and recognize its movement. The incessant activity is not a flaw—it is a phenomenon to be understood. Inner freedom begins not with *suppression,* but with *conscious engagement*: learning to relate to the mind without being dragged by it.

Many people, seeing how wild their minds are, try to rein them in through sheer force of willpower. But willpower, as we know from diets and resolutions, is a short leash—it frays quickly. The horse bucks harder when you grip tighter.

Because pure observation is unstable at first, contemplative traditions offer a simple form of guidance: anchoring attention in the breath. This is not control born of force, but training born of care.

Mounting the Horse: The Discipline of Meditation

You now understand the nature of the wild horse—restless and untamed. You know that fighting it with willpower is futile. So how do you begin? How do you mount this horse without being dragged by it?

The first step of meditation is not suppression but *intentional direction.* Don't try to silence the mind. Train it firmly, gently, and consistently. We do not let the horse roam where it pleases; we give it a field—small, safe, deliberate. That field is the breath.

You take your seat and begin to watch the breath all the way in and all the way out. When the mind wanders—and it will—you notice it and bring it back. Again and again. This is not an act of violence toward the mind; it is an act of education. You are teaching it discipline, and gently restoring rightful mastery.

At first, the mind resists. It tests every boundary. But over time, the reins no longer feel heavy, and a quiet shift occurs. The horse that once *bolted* now walks beside you. The mind that once *enslaved* now reflects.

Here, the distinction between focus and awareness becomes essential:

- **Focus:** the anchor—the breath, mantra, or sensation—the home you return to.
- **Awareness:** the wider consciousness that notices when the mind strays and gently brings it back.

Together they form the rhythm of meditation: the *focused return* and the *gentle noticing.* Each return strengthens awareness; each moment of awareness deepens calm. Slowly, the mind begins to trust the guide.

These short practices open the door. Consistency matters more than *duration* at first—but over time, duration begins to matter too. Twenty minutes daily, or even longer, allows the practice to move from calming moments to transformative change. Deep meditation, done steadily, is what *rewires* the mind at its roots.

The practice was never about forcing the mind into silence, nor about indulging its every whim. It is about discipline balanced with kindness—creating a small field of focus and gently returning to it until stillness *blooms* on its own.

A mind at rest becomes a *wellspring* of calm. A tamed mind becomes an extraordinary *instrument* to serve the world. That is true freedom—to use the mind when you wish, and in the way you wish.

The Contemplative Self in Action

The Contemplative Self has the capacity to remain still while the mind screams for action—letting every thought arise and pass without obedience or opposition. This will does not fight the mind; it simply refuses to serve it. It is steady, clear, and profoundly still.

From this seeing, a new relationship with the mind begins. Thoughts are no longer *commands;* desires are no longer *destiny.* You recognize that suppression only reshapes *bondage*—one compulsion replacing another. Real strength lies not in overpowering the mind, but in understanding it. The Contemplative Self draws power not from force, but from *clarity.*

Meditation is training for life and isn't an escape from life. The Contemplative Self is not a recluse in a cave, but one who lives amidst responsibility with a mind that is calm, tamed, and directed.

A trained mind becomes a reliable servant. It no longer reacts to every stress; it remains steady. In professional life, this means wiser decisions, free from ego or restlessness. In personal life, it means deeper presence—listening without needing to fix, caring without being consumed.

By learning to be still, you act more effectively. By letting go, you gain power. The wild horse of the mind, once untamed, becomes a graceful companion. You are now ready to ride with steadiness, purpose, and freedom.

This is the foundation of the final stage of the journey.

From Doing to Being

This marks a paradigm shift. In earlier stages, meditation was something to be squeezed into free time, a relief from the day's demands. Now, life itself is reframed. The focus is no longer on what to *do* with the day, but on how to *be* through it. Work, service, and duties become intervals—like stepping outside to meet a client before returning home. *The home is meditation; action is a visitor.*

When meditation becomes a way of life, the fruits ripen. Confidence grows that life truly flows from the *inside out.* The light at the bottom of the lake is seen more often, resulting in true rejuvenation. As a result, practicing non-attachment becomes natural, and the mind no longer clings to patterns or validation. Needs lessen, calm deepens, and joy becomes abundant, steady, and unbroken.

The Geometry

Length—Extent of Engagement (Score: 9)

The non-attachment practitioner acts with full engagement, but the mind still *evaluates*—"is this right, is this needed?" That subtle checking creates *micro-friction.* The contemplative one moves from deliberate service to *flow.* When the mind is silent, you don't act because you "should"; you act because the situation asks for it. The friction of right versus wrong is replaced by the clarity of what is. Engagement becomes frictionless and instantaneous.

Width—Scope of Identification (Score: 9)

The person of non-attachment is ready to serve, but bound by moral grooves. Compassion is available, but channeled only toward what is "righteous" or "deserving." Judgment acts as a *gatekeeper* to the heart. The heart is generous, but it has conditions. Righteousness is still the "price of admission."

The practitioner of meditation removes the gatekeeper. In silence, you see the *being* behind the *behavior.* The heart stays available—even when firmness is required. It becomes *less conditional.* The expression of care may differ (firmness for one, gentleness for another), but the availability of care is total.

Depth—Source of Stability (Score: 9)

The non-attached individual finds peace by lightening the load—acting without the weight of results. But they still rely on action to access that peace.

At this stage, Depth undergoes its most fundamental shift. Every earlier source of stability—competence, integrity, space, meaning, calm, independence from outcomes and role—was still, in some sense, a protection against disturbance. Peace was something the person moved toward, maintained, or cultivated. Here, for the first time, peace is discovered as a *pre-existing condition.* The mind's own stillness, *uncovered* through sustained attention, reveals that Well-Being does not need to be produced—it needs to be uncovered. Depth no longer *defends* against the world. It *generates* from within.

The Volume of Well-Being: 9 × 9 × 9 = 729

The Insight: We have moved from 512 to 729. By dropping the heavy armor of "Duty" and "Judgment," and discovering the internal spring, we have unlocked a massive reservoir of Well-Being. We are close to the final potential.

Tools for the Contemplative Self

Meditation, over time, must shift from an *activity* to a *way of life.*

1. **The Formal Practice: The 20-Minute Sit** You cannot tame a horse in 30 seconds. You need time.

    - **The Commitment:** Two sittings of 20 minutes daily (start from 3 minutes and work your way up).

- **The Method:** Anchor on the breath. Count "1" on the inhale, "2" on the exhale, up to 10. Repeat.
- **The Goal:** Not "silence," but "steady return."

2. **The Micro-Practice: The "Gap"** Life is filled with empty micro-moments: red lights, elevators, waiting for coffee.
    - **Old Habit:** Check phone (Distraction).
    - **New Habit:** Watch three breaths (Centering). These "Gaps" bridge the formal practice into daily life.
3. **The Mindset: "Not Now"** When the mind screams for attention with a worry or a plan during meditation, do not fight it. Simply say: "Not now." You are not rejecting the thought; you are prioritizing the silence.

The Structural Limit: The Final Dualism

We have reached 729. The mind is tamed. The heart is wide. The inner spring is flowing. Why is it not yet 1000?

Because of *Duality*. There is still a "Me" enjoying the "Spring."

- I am the *Rider* taming the Horse.
- I am the *Witness* observing the Silence.
- I am drinking from the inner *source.*

As long as there is an Observer separate from the Observed, there is the subtlest of resistance. The Observer is a boundary. There can still be a faint effort in maintaining separateness—a tiny, silent tension in remaining "someone" alongside the whole. This separation is the final, thinnest *veil.* To bridge the gap from 729 to 1000, even that must dissolve.

Summary: The Contemplative Self

Here, we find *stillness in motion.* Engagement is refined into awareness. Identity expands into oneness. And stability finally finds its root in inner quiet. The Contemplative Self has begun to taste the freedom that lies beyond effort. Meditation has ripened into life itself: breath, silence, and action flowing as one.

At this stage something begins to shift in how a person moves through the world. It is not dramatic. It does not announce itself. But those around them begin to notice—and eventually the person notices too. Certain qualities that were previously intermittent begin to stabilize. Not as achievements. Not as practices. As natural expressions of a geometry that has found its depth.

This is how the Contemplative Self manifests:

- **Clarity**—Seeing things as they are, not as the ego paints them.
- **Calmness**—Being the still point in a storm, radiating peace.
- **Contentment**—Finding satisfaction in the present, not in endless seeking.
- **Compassion and Caring**—A mind freed from self-concern is available for others.

This is the doorway to the final stage—where the practitioner grows less identified with doing, and something quieter begins to emerge. Contemplation isn't about silencing the mind; it's about seeing it clearly and returning, kindly, again and again. Each gentle return to your anchor is a vote for freedom. Over time, the wild horse learns trust. Attention returns more quickly. Silence becomes less foreign. What began as a few unstable breaths becomes a steadier home.

Closing Note and Invitation: The Silence Before the Question

You have traveled a long way from the initial friction of inertia.

You moved from Inertia to Ambition, refined it through Ethics and Contribution, and harmonized it through Contentment. You then reduced friction through Non-Attachment—and now, you have steadied the instrument through Contemplation.

You have reached the shores of the inner lake. The sediment has settled. The water is clear. The wild horse of the mind finally trusts the rider. In this stillness, you might feel that you have arrived. The struggle is over. The noise has stopped.

But this silence is not yet the destination. It is the preparation. We cleared the noise so we could finally hear the hum of the one last resistance remaining. The resistance of Identity. The limit is no longer the Horse. It is the Rider.

To reach the final potential, we must turn the inquiry onto the one who is holding the reins.

Who is the Rider?

Chapter 8

The Geometry of Self-Inquiry

This is the culmination of your journey: the work of self-inquiry. What this chapter explores is the investigation of the very sense of "I" that has been present through every stage of this map.

A Note on the Shift: Up until now, we have been refining the picture—adjusting our actions, our ethics, and our focus. Now, we begin to turn the camera around to look at the *photographer.* This shift from "fixing the world" to "inquiring into the self" can feel disorienting. That is natural. We are leaving the solid ground of "doing" for the unbounded space of "being." You do not need to force understanding here; simply stay open to the inquiry.

The Gears of the Inner Lock

Every journey of awakening is like opening a lock with interlocking gears. Each must align perfectly before the next can move. If the Geometry helped us map our expansion, the Lock helps us understand the mechanism of our bondage.

1. **Circumstance:** The belief that peace depends on the world.
2. **Outcome:** The belief that worth depends on results.

3. **Ethics:** The stability found in living with coherence.
4. **Service:** The expansion of identity from "me" to "we."
5. **Contentment:** The peace that comes from "enoughness."
6. **Attitude:** The freedom of acting without clinging.
7. **Mastery of Mind:** The stillness that anchors Well-Being within.

Now, with these gears aligned, the mechanism falls still. Only the innermost gear remains: *Identity.* This final gear is the most subtle of all. It cannot be turned by effort or discipline, only by *seeing.*

Every practice so far has *purified* the instrument; this one *examines* the player. Who is the "I" that acted? Who is the "Rider" we left in the last chapter? As this inquiry deepens, you discover that the "I" you have taken yourself to be—the doer, the thinker, the experiencer—was never the true Self. It was a *reflection* dancing on the surface. The outer gears dealt with motion; this one reveals *stillness.* The outer gears built excellence; this one reveals *essence.*

The End of the "I": The Dissolution of the Ego

The ego has been the resistance through every stage of the journey:

- Challenged by the practice of non-attachment
- Quieted by the practice of contemplation
- Dissolved by the practice of self-knowledge

The ego is not a separate entity—it is a bundle of thoughts and identifications taken to be "me," mistaken for a center. Its "death" is the realization that what seemed to be "me" was never truly there.

The Gold and the Ornament: Think of gold and the ornaments made of it. A bangle, a necklace, and a ring each have a name, a form, and a function. We grow attached to them, believe they are separate, and compare them. "My bangle is better than your ring." But stripped of form, there is no bangle. There is only gold.

So too with us. As long as we identify only with the ego—with our name, form, and fleeting circumstances—we live bound by *limitation.* But when we awaken to our *essence,* we recognize that we are not just the ornament but the gold itself: eternal, unbounded, and *whole.* Liberation is the recognition that while your form (body, personality, role) is the ornament, your substance is Awareness.

The Path of Inquiry

How do we find this gold? Through two complementary practices: Neti-Neti and Self-Inquiry.

1. Neti-Neti ("Not This, Not This") One central method is peeling back the layers of false identification.

- "I am not my body." (I watch it change).
- "I am not my thoughts." (I watch them come and go).
- "I am not my roles." (They are temporary).

Think of a movie. For two hours, you cry and laugh because you think you are the character. Then the lights come on, and you realize you were always the audience, safe in your seat. Now take that one step further: what is the audience watching on? You are the *screen.* The fire in the movie does not *burn* the screen. The water in the movie does not *wet* it. The tragedy does not *hurt* it. You are the screen on which the movie of "my life" appears—the space in which both the "Rider" and the "Horse" arise.

2. The Direct Path: "Who Am I?" A more direct approach, developed within the same tradition, is Self-Inquiry—tracing the 'I'-thought back to its *source* rather than adopting new beliefs.

Every thought you have begins with *I.*

- *I* want. *I* fear. *I* think. But we rarely stop to ask: Who is this *I*?

When a thought arises (e.g., "I am worried about the future"), do not analyze the worry. Instead, turn the attention inward and ask: "To whom does this worry appear?" The answer is: "To me." Then ask: "Who am *I*?"

Do not answer with words. Simply let the mind turn *backward* to look for the source of the *I.* Like a diver following a bubble stream to the bottom, trace the sense of "me" back to where it arises. Eventually, the mind dissolves into the silence of the *Heart.*

The Qualifications for Liberation

Four qualities that ripen naturally through the journey prepare the seeker for this final step: the ability to distinguish *screen from movie;* the ability to enjoy the movie without needing to control the script; the calm mind built through contemplation; and the genuine longing for freedom that kept you reading this far.

The Liberated Self in the World

Liberation is not *escape.* The liberated one still meets joys and sorrows, but no longer as a *prisoner* of them. The inner world is like a still lake; life's events move across it as passing ripples.

What began to stabilize in Contemplation now flows without effort:

- **Clarity**—seeing reality as it is.
- **Calmness**—a mind undisturbed by *storms.*
- **Contentment**—wholeness without *seeking.*
- **Compassion and Caring**—a spontaneous love and service flowing without effort.

Such a person *radiates* peace. Their presence calms, their actions serve, their words guide. Such a one may live quietly, or they may transform entire societies—but in either case, life is no longer fueled by *seeking.* It flows naturally, like a note played perfectly without striving.

The map you have followed has now brought you here—to the end of seeking, and the beginning of true living. This is liberation: not withdrawal, but life lived as *effortless presence.*

The Geometry

This is the geometry of boundless being. This is not a personality achievement or a fleeting state; it is the structural resolution that occurs when identity itself is seen through.

Length—Extent of Engagement (Score: 10)

Action continues, but without a *doer* behind it. The Liberated Self moves through the world—eating, speaking, working—yet the sense of "I am acting" has vanished. Life's movements arise as naturally as waves on the sea. Engagement flows *continuously,* without friction or fatigue.

Width—Scope of Identification (Score: 10)

The circle of identity expands until there is no circumference left. The Liberated Self recognizes all beings as expressions of the same consciousness. Compassion is not an emotion but a *fact of perception.* There are no "others." Love, now without *opposite,* radiates silently in every direction.

Depth—Source of Stability (Score: 10)

The Liberated Self no longer relies on favorable circumstances, outcomes, or even inner states for Well-Being. Peace is not *experienced within* the Self—the Self *is* peace. Joy and sorrow come and go like weather across a vast sky that is never disturbed.

This is not a further point on the same scale. It is the recognition that the one who was *climbing* the *scale* was itself a construction. Every earlier source of Depth was something the person developed, cultivated, or *discovered.* Here, the one who was doing the developing is *seen through.* What remains is not peace as a state that the self inhabits—it is peace as the nature of awareness itself, prior to experience and unchanged by it. The geometry is complete: not because all ten levels have been stacked, but because the structure and the one who built it have *merged* into the same ground.

Volume of Well-Being = 10 × 10 × 10 = 1000

Summary: Length merges into Presence. Width becomes Universality. Depth turns into Infinity. It is the symmetry of freedom itself.

Closing Note: The Lock is Open

All gears have now turned. The lock has opened—not outward into the world, but *inward* into silence. What it reveals is not a hidden jewel to be owned, but an open sky that was always there.

The gears of Circumstance, Outcome, Ethics, Service, Contentment, Attitude, Mind, and Identity have each played their part. They refined action, deepened awareness, and *dissolved the doer.* Now there is no mechanism left to turn. No key to hold. No door to guard. Only spaciousness remains—vast, silent, and still. The seeker and the sought have merged into the same *stillness.*

The Geometry is complete.

Epilogue

The Geometry of an Ordinary Life

You have now walked through the full arc of Well-Being—from inertia to ambition, from ambition to balance, from balance to stillness, and finally toward clarity.

Along the way, you saw how action, ethics, contribution, contentment, attention, and inquiry reshape life. First from the *outside in.* Then from the *inside out.*

Each movement expanded the geometry of living: extending engagement, widening care, and deepening stability.

But maps, however precise, are only half the journey. The other half is *lived*—slowly, unevenly, often without knowing what stage we are in while we are in it.

What follows is not theory. It is simply how this arc unfolded in my ordinary life.

A Life That Coasted (Inertia)

I was raised in Chennai, in a family where ethics and contribution were part of the air we breathed. I studied well, got into engineering, and came to Canada on a scholarship for my Master's.

In hindsight, this was a form of Inertia—in the strict sense of Newton's First Law: an object in motion continues in motion unless acted upon by an external force.

I did not do much to alter my trajectory. I coasted. I did what was expected, stayed safe, aligned with the culture, and drifted with the current. I did not push against life; I let it carry me.

When Fire Finds Fuel (Ambition)

My first job at Bell Northern Research Labs lit the fire. For the first time, I was living on my own terms—earning, choosing, *becoming*.

These were years of genuine abundance. Not just material abundance, though that was present too—the first salary, the first indulgences, the quiet satisfaction of paying my own way. More than that, it was the abundance of becoming. I was reading voraciously: biographies, philosophy, religion and spirituality across traditions, psychology, and neuroscience—drawn by a single question: why are we the way we are? I deepened my love of classical music. I developed friendships that have lasted decades. I performed well, received recognition, earned promotions—and genuinely enjoyed each one.

And then there was Vini. Meeting her, proposing to her, marrying her—these belong to this chapter of life.

Ambition created the conditions. It created the independence. It created the freedom. It created the confidence. It created the sense that life was opening rather than closing. I would not trade those years for anything.

The engine of Ambition, when it first runs, is a beautiful thing. It is *directional energy*—the feeling that you are moving toward something and that the movement itself is meaningful.

Then ambition found a new fuel: money.

These were stock-market years. My mind attached itself to charts, trades, and calculations. The engine that had once run on curiosity and growth began running on *accumulation.* Outwardly, life looked excellent. Inwardly, something *essential* was being lost.

I learned, firsthand, that outer gain—even when successful—can quietly *erode* inner peace. This was my first clear signal: the material game, even when it works, does not deliver what the heart most wants.

Contentment Inhabited (Phase 1)

From Ottawa, the next chapter took us to Dallas.

We had built what most people would recognize as an excellent life. A beautiful home. Wonderful friends—the kind you discuss cricket, culture, philosophy, and life with late into the evening. Sayuj had been born. I had come out of the stock market years, settled into a comfortable rhythm, and was living what is fairly called the American dream: house, cars, an excellent job, an abundant social life, a comfortable and predictable cadence to the days.

And it was good. Genuinely good. I want to be honest about that—this was not a life of quiet desperation. It was a life of real warmth and real pleasure.

But around 2002, something shifted beneath the surface. Life had plateaued—not because anything had gone wrong, but because everything had gone right in a way that felt complete. A life extrapolated in this rhythm felt *limiting.* Not painful. Not broken. Simply—not enough. Not aligned with something deeper that I could feel but not yet name.

I started feeling the limits of materialism from the inside. The house, the cars, the comfortable rhythm—these were genuinely good things. But I began to sense that they were not the point. I wanted to spend time with my parents. I wanted more time for reading, for practicing spirituality, for letting life slow down enough that I could actually *inhabit* it rather than move through it efficiently. I wanted to make it count.

What I did not yet understand—and would only realize much later—is that *time* was not the missing ingredient. I believed then what many people believe: that financial freedom, or a different rhythm, or fewer obligations would finally release me to pursue what mattered most.

The daily routine in Dallas, though genuinely comfortable and not difficult at all, felt constraining in a specific way. I still had to go to work, return at five, navigate the rhythm of house, chores, and shopping. By the end of the day, the space for deeper engagement felt squeezed to nothing. I wanted time. I thought time was what spirituality required.

What I could not yet see was that spirituality is not an activity that requires scheduling. It is an *attitude* that can be practiced anywhere. The daily context I was trying to escape was actually more useful than any amount of free time, because it was precisely there that my dependencies and attachments were most visible.

The difficult colleague. The interrupted evening. The ordinary Tuesday.

These were already showing me exactly where I was still *reactive,* still *attached,* still *conditional.* But I did not have the eyes to read them that way yet. I thought I needed a different life. What I actually needed was a *different relationship* to the life I already had.

That insight would come. But not yet. So we moved back to India—and it is worth saying that the move was never mine alone to make. Vini did not share the same restlessness with Dallas or feel the pull toward India for the same reasons I did. But she brought her own genuine enthusiasm for what the move could offer—time with family, a different pace, a life we would build together in a place that mattered to both of us. Without her equal interest and willingness, the move would not have happened. It was a shared decision, made for different but compatible reasons.

Contentment Sought (Phase 2)

And India gave us real gifts. Time with my parents, years I will always count among the most precious of my life. Friendships formed there that remain among our closest today—people we discuss ideas with, laugh with, and return to across decades. Shreyas was born during this time, and those early years with both boys in that context were irreplaceable.

Work was harder. The cultural differences were real, and I had also made a conscious choice to prioritize family time over professional advancement. I made peace with that tradeoff, though not without some friction.

The spiritual reading deepened. I explored Vedanta more seriously, read more widely, spent more time in reflection. But I was *reading about spirituality* more than *living it.* The understanding was growing. The daily practice was not yet rooted.

Then around 2012, the same restlessness returned—that familiar signal that the current arrangement had reached its natural limit. This time I listened more boldly. I quit my job. I began teaching children logic and programming—work that felt genuinely meaningful. I returned to coding for its own sake rather than as a profession.

And in what remains one of the most unusual and wonderful decisions Vini and I made together, we withdrew Sayuj and Shreyas from their regular school and enrolled them in a US-based online program, teaching them ourselves.

Those two years were extraordinary. With the reclaimed time, we did things that mattered more—not dramatically, not heroically, but genuinely. The pace of life finally matched the pace at which we wanted to live it.

It was Sayuj and Shreyas themselves who eventually pointed toward the next movement. They found the American pedagogical approach more engaging and wanted the experience of middle and high school in the US. Vini and I discussed it, recognized the opportunity it represented for them, and made the decision to return.

Across these twelve years—from Dallas to Bangalore and back—I moved from one form of contentment to another, and then outgrew both. The materialistic contentment of Dallas plateaued and sent me searching. The relational and intellectual contentment of India nourished me but did not fully root a daily spiritual practice. I read more. I understood more. But the understanding had not yet become lived experience.

That gap—between *knowing* and *living*—is what the next chapter of life would begin to close.

The Quiet Weight of Responsibility (The "Ravi" Phase)

The return to the US was not a single shock. It was a series of adjustments that accumulated quietly until the weight became difficult to carry.

We had grown accustomed to a particular way of living in India—not extravagant, but spacious. A 3,300 square feet home. Services readily available. A community where the children could run freely, where neighbors knew each other, where life had a natural social rhythm that did not require planning or driving. The boys had grown up with other children all around them—in the community, in the lanes, in each other's homes at any hour. Friendship was ambient. It did not need to be scheduled.

In the US, everything that had been easy became effortful. Suddenly, things were tight in a way they had never been before.

The children adjusted to the academics well enough—the pedagogy suited them, which had been part of the reason for the move. But adjusting to the social culture of American schools was harder and lonelier than we had anticipated. Making genuine friends took time. The easy *ambient* friendship of their Indian childhood was gone. Meeting friends now required driving, coordinating, planning—and so it happened mainly on weekends. Life became highly structured around activities, *schedules,* and logistics. The spaciousness we had known in India—of time, of community, of unplanned connection—contracted sharply.

And unlike the earlier moves, there was no exit available. We had brought the children here for their education. We could not move again. Whatever the constraints were, we would have to live within them.

Vini's visa did not permit her to work. She channeled her energy into pottery—her passion—and she was good at it, and it gave her something real. I knew this. I was glad for her. And yet I felt a sharp pang of *envy* that I am not proud of. "Why is she free to explore while I am chained to duty?"

The combination of financial constraint, time constraint, the children's social adjustment, the loss of the easy rhythm we had built in India, and the absence of any visible exit—all of it accumulated. There seemed to be no slack anywhere.

The joy of Contribution *dried up.* Life became a burden. I was still doing the right things—but without the *nourishment* that once came with them. For a while, I did not see a way through.

Enoughness, Recovered

The turnaround came from a simple internet search. I looked up income percentiles and realized I was in the top 20%.

That single fact dissolved a guilt I had been carrying quietly—the feeling that I was not contributing enough. It gave me the confidence to speak honestly with Vini.

We sat down and looked at reality together—not *defensively,* but *clearly.* The disparity between our expenses and our income was visible on paper. We made a quiet decision—Well-Being over indulgence, time together over travel, Standard of Life over Standard of Living.

Vini continued her pottery. That mattered deeply—not as a compromise, but as a *priority.* The studio gave her what the geometry describes: expertise built slowly, friendships formed naturally, recognition earned genuinely, and the quiet joy of teaching others. Watching her thrive reminded me what nourishment actually looked like.

I negotiated my own small freedoms—walks, reading, and eventually the gym, which we began attending together. Expenses came down. The rhythm simplified.

Something shifted when we stopped waiting for life to become *more* and started *inhabiting* the life we already had. We began smelling the good life again—Sunday mornings with our boys, evenings that were not scheduled, the particular companionship of two cats named Shifu and Po who arrived and promptly claimed the household.

At work, the urgency to climb quieted. I stopped measuring myself against the next role and started finding satisfaction in what was already in front of me—deepening expertise, building real relationships, delivering excellence without needing an audience. Friendships strengthened. Weeks felt less compressed.

Enoughness returned.

It was during this time, between ages 47 and 50, that I changed my WhatsApp profile to a picture of seven stones balanced perfectly, with the caption: "Balance is beautiful."

And yet, I also felt its *limit.* I wanted to deepen my spiritual practice, but I couldn't break through. The balance was too *fragile* to disturb. That was where things stood when my fiftieth birthday arrived.

Stillness Enters the Picture

For my fiftieth birthday, Vini gave me a ten-day meditation retreat at the Sivananda Ashram in upstate New York. Until then, I had studied Vedanta philosophy, but I had never learned to meditate deeply.

Meditation changed the equation.

Sitting for just twenty minutes twice a day gave me a *charge* I hadn't known was available. For the first time, I was no longer running on *deficit*—drawing from reserves that were already depleted. The practice created a quiet *surplus.* Something was being *replenished* from within rather than borrowed from circumstances.

From that surplus, something shifted in how I related to life's demands. Instead of waiting for conditions to improve—for retirement, for fewer disturbances, for the perfect environment to practice equanimity—I began to see that the material in front of me was already the practice.

The difficult colleague. The unexpected bill. The interrupted morning. These were not obstacles to spiritual growth. They were its *curriculum.*

The question changed from "When will life settle down so I can go deeper?" to "Can I meet whatever arrives right now, fully and without flinching, using this inner charge as my source?"

That reorientation is what gave rise to the "Chef's Kitchen" insight. I could work hard—but with a fundamentally different internal attitude. The kitchen was already open. The orders were already arriving. The only question was whether I could cook from *surplus* rather than *strain,* and release each dish without waiting for the review.

Work no longer drained me. It *purified* me.

Service no longer competed with stillness. It *deepened* it.

Where I Stand Now

I am not enlightened. I have not fully mastered non-attachment, but I am experiencing its benefits. I meditate consistently—twice daily, without exception. Meditation was the *tool* that made the move from Contentment to Non-Attachment possible—it gave me a source within to recharge and revitalize, so that I could open the kitchen and serve without depletion. But having the tool is not the same as having fully *inhabited the stage.* Non-Attachment is where I live more often than not—but not yet always. Meditation sustains the movement. It has not yet become a *way of life* in the deepest sense. The sitting is consistent. The living is still *catching up.*

I feel a quiet *fearlessness* now. I know that if I were blindfolded and dropped in Timbuktu, I would go about doing exactly what I do today: meditate, reflect, and be open to serve whatever context I find myself in. I do not need a "backpack" of status or security to be okay.

If I were to describe my current geometry *honestly,* it is 7 × 7 × 7 = **343.**

A beautiful number. And also a humbling one—because it reveals that 65% of the potential still remains.

That does not discourage me. It *excites* me.

An Invitation

Why share this story? Not to impress—but to *reassure.*

My life followed this arc almost to the letter. It is not a theory; it is a lived path. This is not a *heroic* life. It is an *ordinary* one. Deadlines. Mortgages. Jealousies. Repairs.

And yet, within this ordinariness, Well-Being has unfolded. If these shifts have been possible for me, they are possible for you.

Begin where you are. The geometry does not require a perfect starting point—only an *honest* one. Breathe. Observe. Serve. Reflect. Return.

Well-Being is not something to be earned. It is something to be *uncovered.*

The journey is not about constructing a better self—but about resting, more often and more fully, in the awareness that has been quietly present all along.

Appendix

The Architecture of Depth

A note on this appendix: Throughout this book, the Depth dimension has been described through lived experience—how it feels to live at each stage, what it enables, and where it remains vulnerable. This appendix offers a complementary view: the structural logic beneath those descriptions.

Depth is not a single quality that simply becomes more. It grows through a series of *qualitatively distinct shifts*—each adding a new source of stability, or removing a layer of dependence, in a way that builds on what came before. Two stages—Ethics and Non-Attachment—each contribute two new sources, marking them as the entry points to new arcs of development. All other stages contribute one. The progression of Depth scores therefore follows: 1 → 2 → 4 → 5 → 6 → 8 → 9 → 10 (the *double steps* at Ethics and Non-Attachment reflecting their two simultaneous sources).

The Ten Levels of Depth—What Changes and Why

Stage	New source(s) of stability—and what remains conditional
Inertia (1)	No independent source. *Peace is borrowed from circumstances entirely*—it arrives when conditions cooperate and dissolves when they do not. Stability is a *passenger,* not a *driver.*
Ambition (+1)	Competence—the confidence earned through taking responsibility and producing results. Genuinely more stable than passivity, but still *tethered* to outcomes. Peace rises and falls with the *last result.*
Ethics (+2)	Two sources arrive together. First: *integrity*—the steadiness that arises when action aligns with values, removing the friction of self-betrayal and guilt. Second: *inner space*—the lightness created by non-harm and moderation, which reduces the metabolic and cognitive cost of living. Integrity raises the *floor.* Space lowers the *noise.* This is why the gain at this stage is double.

Contribution (+1)	Meaning—the experience that one's effort matters beyond oneself. Less fragile than outcome-dependence, but still *conditionally anchored*: it *wobbles* when appreciation or visible impact is absent.
Contentment (+1)	*Calibrated calm*—the quiet sufficiency of acting in genuine proportion to capacity, without excess or depletion. This is the deepest stability the *self-managed* life can reach. It holds under ordinary pressure, but not yet under the loss of the self's *own arrangements.*
Non-Attachment (+2)	Two sources arrive together, opening the arc of ego-dissolution. First: *independence from results*—a fundamental change in the relationship to outcomes, not merely better tolerance of them. The inner state is no longer *hostage* to whether the action succeeds. Second: *independence from specific role or field*—the practitioner is no longer confined to a particular identity in order to engage fully. A teacher who can wash the floor with the same quality of presence as teaching has freed a subtle but real constraint. Together, these two shifts mean the world does not need to *cooperate,* and the role does not need to be *preserved,* for peace to remain intact.

Contemplation (+1)	The mind's own stillness—discovered through sustained attention rather than constructed through effort. Every earlier source was *protective:* a reduction of friction, a loosening of dependence. This is the first source that is *generative:* peace is no longer produced or maintained. It is uncovered as a *pre-existing condition.* Depth no longer *defends* against the world. It *generates* from within.
Self-Inquiry (+1)	Not a source—because the one who required a source has been *seen through.* When the separate self is recognised as a *construction* rather than a fact, the question of where Depth comes from dissolves with it. Peace is no longer a state the self inhabits. It is the *nature of awareness* itself—prior to experience, unchanged by it, never actually absent.

The Three Qualitative Transitions

Across these ten levels, three transitions are qualitatively different from the others—not just larger steps, but changes in kind.

The first is at Ethics. Here Depth shifts from purely *outcome-based stability* to something that holds even when outcomes disappoint. Integrity and inner space mean that self-respect no longer depends on the world going well. The self has become more autonomous—though it is still *self-managed.*

The second is at Non-Attachment. Here Depth shifts from *managed stability* to *independent stability.* Earlier stages reduced how much the world needed to cooperate. Non-attachment changes the relationship to cooperation altogether. The practitioner acts fully, but the inner state is no longer defined by results or by the role in which they act. This is the first genuinely *post-ego* movement in the progression.

The third is at Contemplation. Here the direction of stability reverses. Every level up to this point was about *protecting* or *insulating* the inner state from disturbance. Contemplation discovers that peace was present before the protection was needed. Stability becomes *generative* rather than *defensive*—a quality of awareness itself, not of how well the self has been managed.

Self-Inquiry is not a further transition on the same arc. It is the recognition that ends the arc: the one who was traversing it was never quite what it thought it was.

A Note on How These Levels Relate to the Chapters

This appendix is not a replacement for the chapters. Each chapter describes the full lived experience of its stage—the texture, the tools, the structural limit—in a way no table can replicate.

What this appendix offers is a single clean answer to a question the book raises but does not state explicitly: what is actually changing in Depth as the stages progress? The answer, held consistently across all ten levels, is this: the *source.* At each key transition, a new and *more independent source* of stability becomes available—until, at the end of the arc, the very notion of a source dissolves into something that was *never absent.*

This is the architecture beneath the experience. The chapters describe what it feels like to live at each level. This appendix shows why the structure is built the way it is.

Appendix

The Architecture of Width

Width measures the scope of identification—the answer to the question: how far does "I" extend? At its narrowest, the self is a *defended island.* At its fullest, there is no *circumference* left. Between those two points, identification expands through a series of recognizable stages, each one loosening a boundary that the previous stage treated as natural and necessary.

Unlike Depth, which grows through the discovery of new inner sources of stability, Width grows through the progressive *dissolution of the filters* that restrict care. Each level removes or softens one such filter—though not all at once, and not without effort. The later levels, in particular, are not natural expansions. They are the *fruits of practice.*

The Ten Levels of Width—What Expands and What Still Limits

Note: Some stages span more than one level of Width. Ambition, for instance, encompasses two recognizable expansions—from self to immediate family, and from immediate family to extended circle—which together account for its Width score of 3.

Stage	Scope of identification—and where care still stops
Inertia (1)	Self-centred. Attention circles the self's own frustrations, disappointments, and perceived disadvantages. Empathy exists in principle but is consistently *overridden* by self-concern and fatigue. Care rarely reaches outward in any sustained way.
Ambition (+1)	Immediate family. The circle expands to include spouse and children—those whose wellbeing is experienced as *inseparable* from one's own. Care here can be intense and devoted, but the boundary is sharp. What lies outside the immediate family is either *instrumental* or *irrelevant.*

Ambition (+1)	Extended family and close friends. Parents, siblings, and a small circle of trusted friends enter the field of genuine care. Relationships are valued for themselves, not only instrumentally. But the boundary is still defined by personal history and emotional *proximity.*
Ethics (+1)	Community and neighbors. The ethical commitment to non-harm naturally widens the circle beyond personal bonds to include those nearby—colleagues, neighbors, community members. Care here is *principled* rather than purely personal: others are recognized as *ends,* not *means,* even when there is no emotional intimacy.
Contribution (+1)	Relatable causes and shared purposes. As contribution becomes the engine of engagement, care extends to causes, organizations, and groups whose work resonates with one's values—mentees, professional communities, social causes. The boundary is still *preference-based,* but it has moved from personal relationship to *shared identity and purpose.*

Contentment (+1)	My world—curated and complete. The contented person has built a wide, generous, carefully tended circle: family, community, country, faith, causes. Care flows abundantly within it. But the principle of membership is still *ownership and resonance*: I care for what is "mine," what I have chosen, what aligns with my identity. This is the widest the *ego-organized heart* can comfortably reach. To go further requires not a larger circle, but a different relationship to the act of *drawing one.*
Non-Attachment (+1)	The relatable world—beyond mine, but still recognizable. As preference loses its authority, empathy begins to extend to people and situations that were not chosen and do not belong to the self's circle, but that can still be understood and felt for. The filter of *ownership* has loosened. The filter of relatability has not yet dissolved.
Non-Attachment (+1)	Compassion from a neutral position. Care is now the *default orientation* rather than a response to *affinity.* The practitioner meets a difficult colleague or a stranger's problem with the same availability as a passion project. However, this neutrality is not yet *unconditional:* when something genuinely challenges the practitioner's deeply held values or beliefs, the heart may still close. Compassion is the starting point—but it has a residual limit. This is an honest description of the stage, not a failing.

Contemplation (+1)	Compassion extended to all—including those who oppose. In the stillness of sustained meditation, the *gatekeeper of judgment* is removed. The practitioner sees the *being behind the behaviour.* Care becomes available even toward those whose actions are harmful or whose values are opposed to one's own. This is not passive acceptance of harm—firmness is still possible—but the availability of the heart is total. Crucially, this is a *practiced* and *cultivated* expansion, not a natural one. It is the fruit of consistent, deepening meditation over time.
Self-Inquiry (+1)	Compassion as expression, not practice. At this level, compassion is no longer something the person *extends* or *maintains* or *cultivates.* It is *what they are.* The circle of identity has expanded until there is no circumference left. All beings are recognized as expressions of the same awareness. There are no "others" toward whom care must be directed, because the separation that required direction has dissolved. Love radiates not as an emotion but as a *fact of perception.*

The Key Transitions in Width

Three transitions in the Width arc are worth naming explicitly, because they are qualitatively different from the incremental expansions that surround them.

The first is at Contentment. This is not a transition outward but a recognition of a *ceiling*. The heart at this stage is genuinely wide—wider than most people consciously achieve—but it is *organized around ownership and resonance*. Recognizing this is important, because the warmth and generosity of Contentment can make its structural limit invisible. The move beyond it does not require more love. It requires a different relationship to the *principle of membership*.

The second is at Non-Attachment. Here the organizing principle of care shifts from *affinity to availability*. The question changes from "does this belong to my world?" to "is this life in front of me?" This is the first genuinely *post-preferential* expansion, and it accounts for the double step in Width at this stage—mirroring the double step in Depth—because two distinct filters are loosened: the filter of ownership and the filter of alignment.

The third is at Contemplation. This is where compassion becomes *unconditional in practice*—not merely in principle. Earlier stages could affirm the value of universal care while still being unable to sustain it when challenged. Contemplation, through the direct experience of stillness and the removal of the judging mind's authority, makes the unconditional availability of the heart an actual *lived capacity* rather than an *aspiration.* This is why it requires sustained practice, and why it cannot be rushed or reasoned into.

Self-Inquiry is not a further expansion. It is the dissolution of the one who was doing the expanding. Compassion at this level is not directed outward because there is no longer an inward from which to direct it.

A Note on Width Compared to Depth

Depth grows primarily through the discovery of new inner sources of stability—each stage finding a less conditional anchor for peace. Width grows primarily through the removal of filters on care—each stage loosening one boundary that the previous stage experienced as natural.

This means that growth in Width tends to feel less like *acquisition* and more like *release.* The person does not become more caring in some additive sense. They become less *defended,* less *selective,* less organized around the distinction between "mine" and "not-mine." What was always present—the capacity for care—is simply given more room.

This also means that the later levels of Width cannot be reached through intention alone. A person can decide to be more ethical, to contribute more, to manage their energy better. They cannot decide to experience a stranger's pain as their own, or to feel compassion toward someone who has genuinely wronged them. Those expansions require the inner conditions that the later stages—and particularly sustained meditation—create. This is not a counsel of passivity. It is an accurate description of the *sequence*—and the reason this book does not end at Ethics or Contribution, but continues through Contentment, Non-Attachment, and Contemplation. The later stages are not optional refinements. They are the conditions under which the later levels of Width become *genuinely available.*

As with Depth, this table is an abstraction. The chapters describe what it feels like to live at each level of Width. This appendix shows the structural logic of why each level is where it is, and what specifically changes at each transition.

Appendix

The Architecture of Length

Length measures the extent of engagement—the answer to the question: how fully does the person participate in life? At its lowest, engagement is *sporadic* and mood-dependent. At its fullest, it is pure *presence:* the person does not decide to engage, because there is no longer a separate self that could decline.

The progression of Length across the arc has a structure that is easy to miss if only the scores are observed. For the first six levels, Length is an *effort-based* measure: it reflects the proportion of waking energy consciously directed, and the quality of immersion within that direction. This form of engagement has a natural human ceiling—approximately ten hours of genuinely full immersion within a sixteen-hour waking day—beyond which the system depletes rather than compounds. A score of 6 reflects this honest maximum.

From Non-Attachment onward, something fundamental changes. Length is no longer a measure of directed effort. It becomes a measure of *available presence*—the range of life the person can meet without resistance, without the filter of *preference* deciding what deserves full engagement and what does not. The scores above 6 do not represent more hours or greater intensity. They represent a progressively more open relationship to whatever the moment asks. The cuboid of the self—with its defined faces and sharp edges—begins to become a *sphere:* fewer contact points, less friction, more freedom to roll toward whatever life asks.

The Ten Levels of Length—What Changes and Why

Stage	Nature of engagement—and what still limits it
Inertia (2)	Engagement is sporadic and mood-dependent. Action requires an external spark—encouragement, urgency, fear of consequence—and dissolves when the spark fades. Energy flows into imagining and explaining more readily than into *doing.* The person is present in body but frequently absent in *attention* and *intention.*

Ambition (+4)	Engagement becomes self-directed, sustained, and full. The person organizes their energy around goals, projects, and performance. This is a substantial leap—from reactive participation to deliberate authorship of one's own time. Two things account for the full magnitude of this jump. The first is direction: energy is no longer scattered or withheld but consciously organized toward chosen goals. The second is quantity: the proportion of waking hours directed toward purposeful activity rises dramatically—from the bare minimum of Inertia to approaching the human ceiling of sustained engagement. The quality of immersion is high within chosen domains. The risk is that the engine runs without adequate rest, and that leisure becomes instrumental rather than restorative.
Ethics (-1)	Engagement *moderates* deliberately. The pace slows not from exhaustion but from choice: the ethical commitment to moderation and non-harm extends naturally to the rhythm of work itself. This is not a loss—it is the installation of a *governor* that prevents the system from overheating. The person does less, but what they do carries less internal friction and more genuine presence.

Contribution (+1)	Engagement rises again—but the fuel has changed. Action is now animated by *care* rather than *anxiety*, by *overflow* rather than *proving*. Because the motivation is intrinsically cleaner, the same level of engagement feels lighter. The person can sustain higher output without the accumulative cost that ambitious engagement incurred. The engine runs fast again, and this time it is designed for it.
Contentment (score unchanged, quality transformed)	Effort-based engagement reaches its fullest, most sustainable expression. The person has found the natural rhythm of a life in genuine proportion: fully present within the real limits of human energy, protecting recovery, adjusting when strain appears. The score of 6 here is not the same as the 6 of Ambition—there, it represented a *ceiling strained against*. Here, it is the ceiling fully and sustainably occupied. This is the completion of the *effort-based arc*. Length cannot grow further by doing more. What comes next requires a different mechanism entirely.
Non-Attachment (+2)	The nature of Length itself changes here. Directed effort is no longer the variable. What grows is *available presence*—the range of life the person can meet with full engagement, without the filter of *preference* determining what deserves their full attention. As *role-identity* loosens, the field of engagement widens: the person who previously engaged fully only in chosen roles now brings the same quality of presence to what life assigns. This is why the score rises without any increase in hours or effort. The same energy, now less obstructed by preference, reaches further into life.

Contemplation (+1)	*Engagement becomes flow.* The subtle checking that accompanied even non-attachment—"is this right? is this needed?"—dissolves as the mind quietens through sustained meditation. Action arises not from evaluation but from clarity: the situation asks, and the response comes. There is no *micro-friction* between perception and action, no gap between recognizing what is needed and moving toward it. Engagement is now instantaneous and frictionless—not because the person has become faster, but because the one who was deciding has become *transparent.*
Self-Inquiry (+1)	Engagement without a *doer.* Action continues—the liberated self moves through the world, speaks, works, responds—but the sense of "I am acting" has dissolved. Life's movements arise as naturally as waves on the sea. There is no effort because there is no one making an effort. There is no fatigue because there is no one carrying the weight. Presence is total, continuous, and without remainder—not as an achievement, but as the natural condition when the self that was deciding what to engage with has been *seen through.*

The Pivotal Transition: From Effort to Presence

The single most important structural feature of the Length arc is the transition at Non-Attachment—the point where the measure itself changes. This transition has no equivalent in a straightforward scale of more or less. It is a change in kind, not degree.

Before this transition, every increase in Length required either more time, more intensity, or better management of both. The person worked to engage—consciously directing energy, protecting it from depletion, recovering it when it ran low. Even at the optimized level of Contentment, engagement was something the person organized and maintained.

After this transition, engagement is no longer *organized.* It is *available.* The distinction is between a *dam* that controls the flow of water and a *river* that flows because that is its nature. The dam can be made larger or more efficient. The river does not need to try.

This is why the cuboid image from the Interlude is so precise. The contentment-stage life is a well-made *cuboid:* balanced, proportionate, stable. But a cuboid rests on a flat face—maximum contact with the ground, maximum friction, maximum resistance to movement. It stays where it is placed. It requires significant force to move, and when it does move, it tips awkwardly from one flat face to another. That flat face is the ego's investment in specific roles, preferences, and the world it has constructed as its own. As non-attachment rounds those edges, the structure begins to approach a sphere—and a sphere touches any surface at a single point. Minimum friction. It responds to the slightest incline, rolls freely in the direction life tilts, requires almost no force to move. The sphere is not less substantial than the cuboid. It is more mobile, more available, and far less resistant to the world's calling. The ego-organized life *grips* the ground. The life with reduced ego-friction *rolls* across it.

A Note on Length Compared to Depth and Width

Each of the three dimensions grows through a different primary mechanism. Depth grows through the discovery of progressively more *independent sources* of stability—the question it answers is: "where does my peace come from?" Width grows through the *dissolution of filters* on care—the question it answers is: "how far does my concern naturally extend?" Length grows through the *reduction of resistance* to engagement—the question it answers is: "how much of life am I available to meet?"

This means that Length, uniquely among the three dimensions, has a hard ceiling in its first phase (around 6, representing the honest maximum of sustained human effort) and then resumes growth through an entirely different mechanism in its second phase (the progressive removal of the preference-filter). Readers assessing their own Length should hold both phases in mind: if you are below 6, the path forward involves *directed effort* and better management of energy. If you are at 6, the path forward involves not more effort but *less resistance*—which is a *different kind of work,* and belongs to the chapters that describe it.

As with the Depth and Width appendices, this table is an abstraction. The chapters describe the full lived texture of each stage. This appendix identifies the structural logic of why Length sits where it does at each point in the arc—and what specifically changes at the transition that makes the later levels possible.

Summary and Reflection

At this point in your journey, this geometry may help you gently identify aspects of different stages that speak to your life today. Let it *reflect* you without reducing you.

Stage/Type	Geometry (L x W x D = V)	Essence of the Stage	Dominant Emotion/ Energy	The Structural Constraint	Invitation for Growth
1-Inertia	**2 x 1 x 1 = 2** (Stagnant)	**The Victim.** Blames the world for stagnation. Waits for *perfect conditions* before acting.	Frustration, Envy, Apathy	**Externalization.** Belief that the world must change before "I can."	**Move.** Do one constructive thing today. Replace blame with *initiative.*
2-Ambition	**6 × 3 × 2 = 36** (Volatile)	**The Achiever.** Seeks validation through success. Defines self by progress, accumulation, and recognition.	Excitement, Anxiety, Restlessness	**Conditionality.** Well-Being is entirely mortgaged to external outcomes and status.	**Ethics.** Shift focus from *Winning* to *Rightness.*
3-Ethics	**5 × 4 × 4 = 80** (Principled)	**The Steward.** Lives by values and fairness. Chooses right action even when *costly.* Anchors Well-Being in virtue.	Poise, Integrity, Dignity	**Judgment.** Frustration at unethical people/systems. "Moral Anger" disturbs peace.	**Compassion.** Temper *righteousness* with understanding. Move from *Right* to *Helpful.*
4-Contribution	**6 × 5 × 5 = 150** (Expansive)	**The Giver.** Expands focus from self to service. Works for collective good with energy and care.	Generosity, Purpose, Fulfillment	**"The Silent Ledger."** Subtle scorekeeping ("I give so much..."). Joy depends on appreciation.	**Detachment.** Learn to give for the *joy of giving,* not the return of thanks.

Stage/Type	Geometry (L x W x D = V)	Essence of the Stage	Dominant Emotion/ Energy	The Structural Constraint	Invitation for Growth
5-Contentment	**6 × 6 × 6 = 216** (Stable)	**The Manager.** Lives peacefully in *calibrated balance.* Optimizes for stability, comfort, and predictability.	Calm, Satisfaction, Comfort	**"The Curated Circle."** The "Golden Handcuffs" of comfort prevent further growth or risk.	**Inquiry.** Ask: "Is this it?" Dare to disturb the peace to find the *Truth.*
6-Non-Attachment	**8 × 8 × 8 = 512** (Flowing)	**The Instrument.** *Acts fully but without ownership.* The anxiety of the "Doer" is replaced by the *flow* of service.	Equanimity, Availability, Lightness	**The Impulse.** The mind still *dictates* when and how to act.	**Stillness.** Move from purifying action to silencing the *actor* (Contemplation).
7-Contemplation	**9 × 9 × 9 = 729** (Radiant)	**The Observer.** Discovering the *inner lake.* The mind is tamed; joy is found *within,* independent of the world.	Tranquility, Clarity, Joy	**The Dualism.** There is still a "Rider" enjoying the peace. Separation remains.	**Surrender.** Drop the Observer. Inquire: "Who is the Rider?"
8-Self-Inquiry	**10 × 10 × 10 = 1000** (Infinite)	**The Screen.** Ego *dissolved.* Life flows as *effortless presence.* The seeker and the sought are *one.*	Bliss, Oneness, Silence	**None.** The geometry is *complete.*	**Abide.** Simply *be.*

A Request from the Author

Thank you for reading The Geometry of Well-Being. If this book has been useful to you in any way, I would be deeply grateful if you could take a moment to leave a review on Amazon. Reviews help other readers discover the book and mean more to an independent author than you may realize.

You can also visit geometryofwellbeing.com to learn more about the framework and connect with me directly.

Your feedback helps shape future work.

With gratitude,

Ramesh Srinivasan

About the Author

Ramesh Srinivasan is a Solutions Architect with Unisys, based in Harrisburg, Pennsylvania. Over thirty-five years, he has built software products, services, and solutions across Canada, India, and the United States—a career defined as much by crossing boundaries as by technical craft.

His thinking was shaped by three distinct influences. Vedantic philosophy, encountered early in life, kindled enduring questions about Well-Being and inner freedom. Decades of work in software systems—reasoning about architecture, constraints, and optimization—gave those questions structure and precision. And the experience of living deeply in both East and West, not once but twice, expanded his understanding of what a universal framework for human flourishing might actually look like—one that holds across cultures, responsibilities, and the real challenges life brings.

He lives with his wife Vini and their sons Sayuj and Shreyas. *The Geometry of Well-Being* is his first book.

www.ingramcontent.com/pod-product-compliance
Lightning Source LLC
LaVergne TN
LVHW090517110826
845146LV00003B/885

* 9 7 9 8 9 9 5 6 7 7 6 1 1 *